The Revenge by Aphra Behn

or, A Match in Newgate

Aphra Behn was a prolific and well established writer but facts about her remain scant and difficult to confirm. What can safely be said though is that Aphra Behn is now regarded as a key English playwright and a major figure in Restoration theatre

Aphra was born into the rising tensions to the English Civil War. Obviously a time of much division and difficulty as the King and Parliament, and their respective forces, came ever closer to conflict.

There are claims she was a spy, that she travelled abroad, possibly as far as Surinam.

By 1664 her marriage was over (though by death or separation is not known but presumably the former as it occurred in the year of their marriage) and she now used Mrs Behn as her professional name.

Aphra now moved towards pursuing a more sustainable and substantial career and began work for the King's Company and the Duke's Company players as a scribe.

Previously her only writing had been poetry but now she would become a playwright. Her first, "The Forc'd Marriage", was staged in 1670, followed by "The Amorous Prince" (1671). After her third play, "The Dutch Lover", Aphra had a three year lull in her writing career. Again it is speculated that she went travelling again, possibly once again as a spy.

After this sojourn her writing moves towards comic works, which prove commercially more successful. Her most popular works included "The Rover" and "Love-Letters Between a Nobleman and His Sister" (1684–87).

With her growing reputation Aphra became friends with many of the most notable writers of the day. This is The Age of Dryden and his literary dominance.

From the mid 1680's Aphra's health began to decline. This was exacerbated by her continual state of debt and descent into poverty.

Aphra Behn died on April 16th 1689, and is buried in the East Cloister of Westminster Abbey. The inscription on her tombstone reads: "Here lies a Proof that Wit can never be Defence enough against Mortality." She was quoted as stating that she had led a "life dedicated to pleasure and poetry."

Index of Contents
ACT THE FIRST
SCENE the First
SCENE II
ACT THE SECOND
SCENE the First
SCENE II

SCENE III
ACT THE THIRD
SCENE the First
SCENE II
SCENE III
ACT THE FOURTH
SCENE the First
SCENE II
SCENE III
SCENE IV
ACT THE FIFTH
SCENE the First
SCENE II
SCENE III
SCENE IV
APHRA BEHN – A SHORT BIOGRAPHY
APHRA BEHN – A CONCISE BIBLIOGRAPHY

ACT THE FIRST

SCENE the First

A Street.

Enter **SAM** with Torch, **MR DASHET** raving, followed by **MRS DASHET**.

MR DASHET
Run, you Rogue, run, raise the Street, you Son of a careless Whore: Cry, Stop Thief, stop Thief!

SAM
Which way, Sir?

MR DASHET
A Pox of ways: Sirrah, cry, Stop Thief, I say.

SAM
So we may stop honest men, Sir.

MR DASHET
There's no such thing within the Walls of London, ye Rogue; there's nothing but Knaves, Cheats, Cuckolds and Traytors, Thieves and Pickpockets, tho I be one of the Livery. A Pox of Honesty, my Plate's gone, the Reckoning unpaid, I'm cheated and undone! therefore run, ye Dog, run.

MRS DASHET
Good sweet Husband, have patience.

MR DASHET
Patience! yes, so you advis'd when I found the Alderman and your Ladyship in a civil posture on the red Couch in the Swan. Patience quotha! Pox of your Remedies. Get ye in, here's Company.

[Enter **FOOTMAN** with Flambeau, follow'd by **FRIENDLY** and **WELLMAN**.

WELLMAN
Whe! how now, Mr. Dashit, what inrag'd in Rancor, and the Beauty of the London-bars, your Lady too, in Tears! What's amiss? unfold thy dismal story.

MR DASHET
Onely cheated, robb'd, abus'd, and undone, Sir: that's all, that's all.

[Weeps.

WELLMAN
As how, man! Come, advance thy comely Countenance, and do not let thy sorrowful Snout bedew thy reverend Jerkin. The reason, my hardly honest Dashit.

MRS DASHET
Oh Si, Mr. Trickwell that Knave is this night run away with our great Gallon-Tankard, six silver Boats, a great Salt, besides Spoons and Forks.

MR DASHET
Oh, for some wise man that wou'd but finde 'em out presently!

WELLMAN
Yes, if a wise man cou'd be found out presently.

FRIENDLY
How was this Plate lost? how escap'd he unseen with it?

MR DASHET
Why, an't like ye, Sir, thus: As I understand, that man, man, quoth I? no, rather Monster, that t'other-end-of-the-Town-Villain, nay, I believe that Jesuit in disguise, sent from beyond Sea to ruine honest Citizens; I say, this Heathen Trickwell comes me into my house this evening with a great two-handed Gentlewoman, or some Priest in Petticoats; they call for a Room, pretend to send a Porter for some Ladies of delight, bespeak a Supper, but no Ladies came.

MRS DASHET
My Cockie forgets to tell your Worships, that our house being full, we had no Room emptie but the great Parlor below stairs.

MR DASHET
Hold your peace, hold your peace, I say. Am I a Common-Council-man like to be of the Citie of London, and cannot tell my Tale my self? Get ye in, I say, and look to what's left.

WELLMAN

Well, Sir, on with your Relation.

MR DASHET
Well, Sir, a noble Supper they had of the best in season; I came in, cri'd, Your servant, Gentlemen; ask'd 'em how they lik'd their Wine, and departed civilly: Then enter'd a blinde Harper, cries, Do ye lack any Musick, Sir? He cries, Play: The Harper uncases, the Drawer is nodded out, who obeys, believing he wou'd be private with the Gentlewoman; and 'tis Sam's part, you know, Sir, to wink at things.

WELLMAN
Right and civil.

MRS DASHET
Aye, aye, but he shall answer for that winking at the last day, I'll warrant him.

MR DASHET
Well Sir, having eat the Supper, and Trickwell perceiving none in the room but the blinde Harper, whose Eyes Heaven had shut up from beholding wickedness, opens the Casement to the street, very patiently packs and pockets up my Plate, unnaturally thrusts the woman out of the window, and himself most preposterously with his heels forwards follows. The Harper plays on, bids the empty Dishes much good may do 'em, and plays on still. The Drawer returns, cries, What d'ye lack, Gentlemen? but out, alas, the Birds were flown, Sir, flown. Laments are rais'd.

WELLMAN
Which did not pierce the Heavens.

MR DASHET
Sam cries out; my Wife in the Bar hears the noise, and she bawl'd out; I heard her, and thunder'd; the Boys flew like Lightning, and all was in confusion.

WELLMAN
Well, this must be for some great sins committed; the sins of the Bar and Sellar, unmerciful Bills, and suffisticated Wine, my honest damn'd Vintner:—Repent, oh repent and mend, and be sound.

MR DASHET
Well, I will hang that Rogue Trickwell, and there's an end on't: I'll do't; and so Good night to you, Gallants.

[Exit **MR DASHET** and his **WIFE**, as into their house.

WELLMAN
Well, dear Jack, Good night: I have a Visit to make before I sleep, and will take my leave o'thee. A sound Wench, soft Sleep, and pleasant Dreams, bless thee, my dear Friendly.

FRIENDLY
Not so, I'll see thee safe at home; I dare not leave ye to your self so late; you are warm with Youth and Wine, which may direct you to the undoing of that body of yours which shortly must be blest with chast embraces. These common women will ruine thee, Frank; Faith leave 'em in good time: come, you shall not to a Bawdy-house, I hate 'em.

WELLMAN
I pray for their continuance and increase ere since I thought of Marriage.

FRIENDLY
Prithee why?

WELLMAN
A married man ought to love a Bawdy-house, as English-men love Flanders; wish war shou'd be maintain'd there, lest it shou'd be brought home to their own doors.

FRIENDLY
Thou art a worthy Lad, and brave; but this damn'd Lust has been thy constant daily vice, the onely one thou'rt given to.

WELLMAN
Prithee call it a nightly one: But not to trifle with thee, Faith I am going the way of all flesh.

FRIENDLY
To a Whore?

WELLMAN
One thou callest so, a very Publican and sinner.

FRIENDLY
And canst thou, having such an Object before thy eyes as the fair, the chast Mirinda, whom thou'rt to marry, give thy self up to the loose, the common arms of one who loves thee not but for her interest? Damn her, thou shalt not go. I hate, I nauseate a common Prostitute, who trades with all for gain; one that sells humane flesh, a Mangonist.

WELLMAN
Poor Devils, what wou'd you have 'em do? wou'dst thou have 'em get their living by the Curse of man, the Sweat of their Brows? Egad they dearly earn what we give 'em. Is Charitie grown a sin, or relieving the Poor and Impotent, an offence? And Faith, Franck, where can we bestow our Money better? In Land the Title may be crackt, in Houses they may be burnt, in fine Cloaths they'll wear out, in Wine, alas, our Throats are but short, and our heads weak; but woman, oh dear lovely woman's the lasting true pleasure! Lay it out upon woman, I say, and a thousand to one, some one of them will bestow that on you that shall stick by you as long as you live: They are no ungrateful persons, they'll give Love for Love; do you protest, they'll swear; do you vow, they'll lye; do you sigh, they'll weep; do you give them English Coin, they'll repay you with the French—And they onely sell their Bodies: Do not some of our Sex sell their Souls? nay, since all things have been sold, Honour, Justice, Faith, even Religion, pray where's the dishonour of selling the Pleasures of a womans Bed? Who is't wou'd live and toil, but for a woman? who fights, lies cold and hard in open field, but to gain Wreaths to lay at a womans feet?
And 'tis a truth can be denied of no man:
All things were made for man, and man for woman.
—Give me my Fee.

FRIENDLY

Well, Sir, I see you are resolv'd, and I can onely boast I love Diana better than you do her Sister Marinda.

WELLMAN
Come, wilt thou go with me?

FRIENDLY
Whither?

WELLMAN
To this house of Salvation.

FRIENDLY
Salvation!

WELLMAN
Yes, 'twill make thee repent. Prithee go to the Family of Love, I'll shew thee my Creature, my Natural, my Mistriss, my pretty blue-ey'd Wanton, my honest fond self-hearted Flatterer, my fair-fac'd, sweet lip'd Rogue, that has Beauty enough for her Vertue, Vertue enough for a Woman, and Woman enough for any reasonable man, in my knowledge.

FRIENDLY
What to a Bawdy-house, to visit an impudent Prostitute? Pox on't, 'twill make me hate the Sex. The worst Object the world can shew me, is an immodest vulgar woman.

WELLMAN
No matter, thou shalt go; go as thou lovest me.

FRIENDLY
Well, Sir, I'll go to bring you safely back.

[Exeunt.

SCENE II

SCENE: Draws to a House.

Enter **MRS DUNWELL**, and **TRICKWELL** drunk.

TRICKWELL
Nay, Moll, unreasonable Mary! whe, the whole Prize was not above fortie pound; and hast thou the conscience to snack ten onely for a good word speaking, a little holding the door, and bawding? The device was my own too, the hazard mine, and the hanging may be mine, whilst thou securely filchest under my conduct. Come, the nest of Cups is fair, you Bitch, be contented; you were drunk too into the bargain, Moll. Come, bear a Conscience, Moll, and Heaven will bless our endeavours: besides, Moll, thou hast an honest Calling of Bawding, which brings thee in a pretty Livelihood, Moll; when God knows I trust to nothing but my own indurious slight of hand. Come, give me back the Salt.

[Snatches the silver Salt.

MRS DUNWELL
By Yea and by Nay, Trickwell, I am afraid thou wilt play the Knave, and restore 'em.

TRICKWELL
No, by the Lord, Aunt, Restitution is Catholick; and you know Oracles are ceas'd. Tempus præteritum.—Dost hear, my necessary Evil?—Thou ungodly Fire that burnt Diana's Temple, dost hear? make Corina civil, or by the Lord, Bawd—

MRS DUNWELL
Fire! Gad you are the foulest mouth'd son of a Whore, the profanest railing Raskal, call a woman the most ungodly names! I must confess we all eat of the forbidden Fruit; and for my own part, though I am, as they say, a Bawd that covers a multitude of sins, yet I trust I am none of the wicked that go to Steeple-houses with profane Organs in 'em, ye scurvy sawcie Jack.

TRICKWELL
Who, I rail at thee, my industrious Moll, my subtle Procurer? I rail at thee, my necessarie Damnation? I'll make an Oration in praise of thy Modestie, thou flower of thy Function.

MRS DUNWELL
And I think I have deserv'd it at your hands, Mr. Trickwell; for I have assisted you early and late, up-rising, and down-lying.

TRICKWELL
Thou hast; therefore listen: A Bawd for her Profession is the most honourable of all the 12 Companies; for as that Trade is most worshipful that sells the best Commodities, what must the Bawd be then, my little Moll? For where others sell silk Cloaths, Gold and Silver, Pearls and Diamonds, thou sellest divine Vertue, Virginitie, Modestie, Maiden-heads, Youth and Beautie: And who are her Customers? not Cits, Grooms, Mechanicks, and disbanded Souldiers; but Gentlemen of the best Rank, Knights, Lords, Dukes, and Squires. Thus she lives, keeps the best Company, eats and drinks of the best, and domineers when she's drunk, reigns Queen, Moll, over her adoring Subjects. But hold, here's Wellman and Friendly! what a Pox does his Gravitie in a Bawdie-house?
Enter Wellman and Friendly.

WELLMAN
Come along, yonders the Preface to my Mistriss, her Matron, or Bawd, or what you please. Mrs. Dunwell, your servant.

MRS DUNWELL
Your servant, sweet Sir: Ah, you're a prettie man, to neglect a Creature that loves you thus; introth you are—But well, I'll fetch her to you, Sir.—

[Exit **MRS DUNWELL**.

WELLMAN

Do so, sweet Mrs. Dunwell.—What, Mr. Trickwell, does your Knaveship dare walk the street? Look to't, Mr. Dashit lies in wait for you.

TRICKWELL
The more fool he; I can lie for my self: A Pox of the rich Raskal, 'tis no deceit in me to cheat him; he has cozen'd me of an Estate of some two hundred a year, with his damn'd Reckonings, and then who but honourable Mr. Trickwell, the noble Squire, and soforth, till he had got all my Land in Mortgage; then took the forfeiture, and turn'd me out of doors. I'll plague him for't. But I interrupt your diversion, and will kiss your hands, my noble Patrons.

[Exit **TRICKWELL** with the Plate.

[Enter Dunwell and **CORINA**, she kicking her.

WELLMAN
See, Sir, this the ugly thing you so despise!

FRIENDLY
This!

WELLMAN
This very thing: 'tis but a Dowdie—but she serves.—

FRIENDLY
A Whore this! Vertue defend me, what a lovely woman 'tis!

WELLMAN
Salute her, man, salute her.

FRIENDLY
Salute her! yes, and leave my heart upon her lips.

WELLMAN
Go, salute my friend; this is my friend Corina.

CORINA
I care not for you nor your friends; I'm sure you use me scurvily, because you know I love you: but I shall learn those Arts you men are practis'd in; and scorn, and hate, and hide it, when it serves my turn, as you can do.—I shall—but yet I'm true, true as my Vertue when you first seduc'd it, false as you are, — and yet I love you strangely.—

WELLMAN
Salute my friend, I say—go, you fond fool, clasp his neck round, and press his cheeks to yours; kiss him as you do me, as soft and meltingly: go, you coy tit, I say you shall.
[Kisses him.

FRIENDLY
She'as fir'd me with that touch:—there's Witchcraft in't.

WELLMAN
Come, kiss her again; by Heaven thou shalt, I'll not be jealous on't: kiss her more ardently—So, thou wilt learn in time. Go fetch your Lute, and let him hear ye sing to't.

CORINA
I'm all obedience, Sir, when you command; but I have something heavie at my heart that makes me wish you wou'd excuse me now.

WELLMAN
Go too, I say—what can sit heavie there? I love thee, love thee infinitly, in faith I do, Corina. Here, here's Gold for thee; the Summer's coming on, and thou perhaps wants Toys, as Gowns and Points, and Petticoats. I'll have thee show, Corina, with the best, splendid and gay, my Girl, as is thy Beauty.

CORINA
I'll take this Gold, but 'tis not that I want: methinks of late there is a strange decay of Passion in you; you're not so dearly fond as you were wont, supplying still your want of Love with Gold; your Mirth is forc'd, your Visits cold and short, as Winterdays; and when you speak of Love, you do't with caution. There's some reserve hid in that generous breast, which I wou'd be acquainted with, yet tremble lest you shou'd betray't too soon.

WELLMAN
Corina, you mistake my heart, 'tis thine, intirely thine; but when a Lover's sure, as I am of thy heart, those little assiduities are neglected which onely hoping Lovers use to pay. I am happie now, and have no need of Vows but those of Constancie. Go to your Lute.

CORINA
And have ye none you do designe to marry?

WELLMAN
Fie, you're a fool to think I be so weak; Marry! I scorn that slaverie, whilst I possess all the delights of it with thee, without its plagues and care.—Go to your Lute.

[Exit **CORINA**.

Well, Frank, and how dost thou like my Mistriss? is she not charming? do you blame me now? Introth I lov'd her dearly once, till my Soul shew'd me the imperfections of my bodie, and plac'd my love on a more worthy object, my fair Marinda; which if this Baggage knew, there were no being for me, she wou'd so rave: But faith I think I'm not so criminals as you imagin'd, hah?

FRIENDLY
Yet she's a Whore!

WELLMAN
A Whore! Oh call her a Miss, a Ladie of the Town, a Beautie of delight, or any thing. Whore! 'tis a nauseous name, and out of fashion now to call things by their right names. Is a Citizen a Cuckold? no, he's one of the Liverie: Is a great man a Fool? no, he's weak, or led away: Is a Person of Qualitie pockie? no, but is not well, has got a Surfeit, or so. Come, she is a Mistriss,—but heark, she sings!

[A Song within to a Lute, after which, enters **CORINA**.

FRIENDLY
She's all a perfect Heaven! Oh I adore her!

CORINA
To obey your commands, I sung, my Love, but I had rather you had pardon'd me.

WELLMAN
You are a simple Chit; go, get you gone, and let me go; 'tis late, and I am sleepie.

CORINA
This Language was not wont to come from thee; take heed, and do not cheat my easie Faith: for if you do, perhaps 'twill make me mad; and in my wildness some strange things may do, may ruine both our lives. Take heed; for now I love ye much above 'em both. Come, you shall stay with me to night.

WELLMAN
By no means, my Dear; this Gentleman has vow'd to see me chastly laid.

CORINA
And so ye shall: the Play of Infants shall not be more chast. I have no wish to make him break his Vow, and he shall have a Bed.

WELLMAN
Peace! that offer will offend him; he's a modest man, one of a profest abstinence. Good night.

CORINA
And must you go?

WELLMAN
I must.

CORINA
And will you come to morrow? But oh I did not use to ask such Questions. Will you be sure?

WELLMAN
I will: when did I fail? Good night. Boy, your Flambeau. Good night, Corina.

[He goes out, **FRIENDLY** stays.

CORINA
Why stay you, Sir? you see your friend is gone.

FRIENDLY
Madam, if he knows not how to prize Heaven, I do; and cannot leave the pleasure so soon, at least if you wou'd give me leave to gaze, I dare not say possess, that were a blessing fit onely for the Gods; nor

knows man how to calm it.—That you shou'd throw away such wonderous beautie on the remiss, cold, and insensible!

CORINA
Who is it, Sir, that's so insensible?

FRIENDLY
Death, whither does my passion hurry me? I shall betray friendship of many years, for a flame which a new lust has kindled in a moment.

CORINA
Heavens! are you silent, Sir? what made ye talk of one remiss and cold? who mean ye? Wellman? Oh, if you did—

FRIENDLY
I meant mankinde; for none can merit you.—Is she unchast? can such an one be damn'd? Oh Love and Beautie, you two eldest seeds of the vast Chaos, what strong right ye have even in things divine, our very Souls!

CORINA
Why do you stifle what was so well begun? Unfold; I know you have some meaning, Sir, in what you have to say: Concerns it Wellman?

FRIENDLY
No. Answer me one thing, Madam.

CORINA
I will: for you have something to relate, which I must hear. Demand; I listen.

FRIENDLY
The Question is but rude.

CORINA [Aside]
I care not.—What means he?

FRIENDLY
Are you—You pardon me?

CORINA
I do. There's something in his heart that I must flatter thence. Be confident.

FRIENDLY
And are you then—a—Whore? You said you wou'd forgive.

[Bows.

CORINA

I did: and though that question, yet 'cause I know thou hast some reason for't, I'll answer thee directly, That I am.

FRIENDLY
Are Prostitutes such things, so delicate? Can custom spoil what Nature made so good? I never saw a sweet face vitious: it might be proud, inconstant, wanton, vain.

CORINA
Oh leave, Sir, to philosophize on Beautie, and tell me why you do so.

FRIENDLY
Heavens! why cou'dst not thou be constant?

CORINA
Constant! to what? to whom?

FRIENDLY [To **WELLMAN**]
He has all the Charms of Nature; and to be false to him, was such a sin—

CORINA
Oh Heavens! what base flatterer has traduc'd me? tell me; who dares report I am not true, not true to Wellman? I have been false to Vertue, false to Honour, false to my Name and Friends; but was to Wellman what Heaven is to the Just and Penitent, all soft, all mercie, all complying sweetness.

FRIENDLY
By Heaven, I do believe it; and nere heard a breath that cou'd prophanely say thou wert not: But oh, I thought with reason, if 'twere so, I cou'd not slightly part with such a Jewel, or, Indian-like, barter this real Gold for shining gingling Bawbles. Marinda! Heaven, thou'rt an Angel to her!

CORINA
Enough: I know my doom; that word's enough; and I'm betray'd to ruine!
[Aside]
I will: My heart, thou shalt dissemble this—Go, base false man, that with the name of Friend has play'd the Traytor to the best of men. I know thou injur'st Wellman; or if true, 'twas not thy part to tell it: hadst thou license for such a cruel Tale, thou shou'dst have spar'd it to her that lov'd thy friend. Be gone, I hate thee, and whatsoere thou meants by such a Lye, I scorn thee for't, and think thee much unfit for any gallant friendship: I know 'tis truth, and with the fatal knowledge instruct my heart to break.

[Goes out.

[**FRIENDLY** musing alone, enter peeping **WELLMAN**.

WELLMAN
Tho I do not care for this woman now, yet some dregs of the old haunt of Jealousie remain about me still; and I must see what use my friend and quondam Mistriss makes of this kinde opportunitie.—Hah! alone, and musing!

[Listens.

FRIENDLY
'Twas not well done, indeed, to tell her; but Love was raging in me, and I believ'd I shou'd insinuate with that secret.

WELLMAN
By Heaven, he's caught! Eternal Laughter seize me.

FRIENDLY
'Twas Love! the very first effects of Love were treacherous and ill: Heaven guard me from the rest. Yet I must on:
Let Winter'd Age dully pretend to prove
That Love is Lust; I know no life but Love.

WELLMAN
Is it so, Sweet-heart? how is't? what, is the worst sight the world can produce, a common woman now?

FRIENDLY
Hah! will you go home, Sir? 'tis high bed-time.

WELLMAN
With all my heart, Sir; onely do not chide me. I must confess.—

FRIENDLY [Shaming]
A wanton Lover you have been.

WELLMAN [Shaming agen]
When Love was raging in me.

FRIENDLY
Oh leave your rallying; will you be gone?

WELLMAN
Let Winter'd Age dully pretend to prove
That Love is Lust; I know no life but Love.
Go thy ways for an Apostate; I believe my last Garment must be let out in the seams for you: Is't not so?
But come, I must go serinade Marinda; but take this certain rule along with thee:
Of all the Fools that Ignorance ere nurst,
He that 'gainst Nature wou'd be wise, is worst.

[Exeunt.

ACT THE SECOND

SCENE the First

A Street.

Enter **WELLMAN** and **FRIENDLY**, with **FOOTMEN** with Lights, and men with Musick; as under Marinda's Window.

WELLMAN
Well, Gentlemen, here's the Window of my dear Marinda: 'tis here, my friends, resides that lovely Maid, whose beautie chaces away those lesser fires that did infest my heart. Come, gently touch your strings, and call her forth to bless me ere I go to rest: I'm not half sanctifi'd without a sight.

[They play a little, then a Song.

[Enter **MARINDA** above, in Night-dress, and **DIANA**.

MARINDA
Who's there, my dear lov'd Wellman? This was kinde.

WELLMAN
My generous Marinda! when did I ere approach thee but with kindness, the fondest tenderest part of kindness too? and when I cease to do so, Heaven neglect me.

MARINDA
And me, when I but fear the contrary. Wou'd I cou'd let thee in; but oh I dare not: my Father nicely careful, tho thou'rt mine, mine by a solemn Contract, yet forbids me to entertain thee with that freedom yet.

WELLMAN
But, my Marinda, 'tis a heavenly night, such as was made for Lovers, still and calm; and I have such soft things to whisper to thee, as pains me to conceal. I long to touch thy hand, to catch thy sighs, and lean my head upon thy rising bosome. A freedom now methinks you might allow me: 'tis very hard.

MARINDA
'Tis so; but yet a little suffering, and we may meet with lawful freedom: till when, continue to be true and kinde.

WELLMAN
By Heaven, by all the Stars that shine above, and by thy brighter Eyes, I will be ever true.

MARINDA
I must give faith to what you say; and prithee since, easie Maid, I do believe so soon, in pitie do not cheat me. Here, wear this little Ring; a dying Brother gave it, and bad me never part with it but to him that Love had made my Husband: Wear it thou; for thou'rt my Souls best choice.

[Takes it in his hand, and kisses it.

WELLMAN
Which when I part from, Hope, the best comfort of my life, forsake me.

DIANA
Heavens! what a long tedious Tale of Faith and Troth's here! Cou'd I once see the man I lik'd, I'd have done a thousand fine and more material things by this time.

WELLMAN
Madam, here is a Man, whom if you cou'd but pity—

DIANA
What, my grave Lover Mr. Friendly, who hates a Wencher! no by my Troth, I'm for no such dull Ingredience in a Lover: I love a man that knows the way to a womans bed without instructions. Besides, what shou'd we two do together, get Fools? no, I hate 'em.

WELLMAN
You may be mistaken in your man.

DIANA
I wish I were: Let him but bring it under the hand of any woman who has been kinde to him, and I'll believe him fit to be belov'd by me; till then, I am obdurate.

FRIENDLY
Well, Madam, I'll endeavour to obey you.

DIANA
Let it be quickly then, I hate delays, you know I'm stor'd with Lovers, Sir John Empty will be before-hand with you else; you know he's a spruce Spark, and cannot long lay siege before a heart, but he will force an entrance: he's of my humour too, gay, loves Fiddles, Wine and Women; a fool and rich, oh heavenly Quality! Be wise, Sir, and consider 'em, and learn to whore betimes; you know not what you may come to. Farewel, the day begins to break, and the old man will wake. Good morrow, modest Mr. Friendly.

[Exeunt from the window.

WELLMAN
Good morrow, mad-cap: Come, shall's go to bed?

FRIENDLY
No, I cannot sleep; I'll walk a little.

WELLMAN
And meditate? Farewel, Sir, I'm for rest.

[Exeunt all but **FRIENDLY**.

FRIENDLY
This woman yesterday was charming to me, and now all that she said, seem'd dull and tedious. What a strange change is here! The light comes on; heark how the free-born Birds chant forth their untaught Passions, and in those pretty Notes express their love. They have no Bawds, no mercenary Beds, no politick Restraints, no artful Heats, no faint Dissemblings; Custom makes them not blush, nor Sham afflicts their name. Oh happy Birds, in whom an inborn heat is held no sin! how vastly you transcend

poor wretched man, whom national custom, tyrannous respect of slavish order fetters, calling that sin in us, which in all else is Nature's highest Vertue. But a Whore! now shame forsake me, whither am I fallen, one that my friend has had, to live to be a shameful talk to men!

[**WELLMAN** returns.

WELLMAN
I have a mind to know whether Friendly goes to Corina; when I am absent, 'tis with some regret I think he shou'd; but present, it so pleases me to see his modesty in love, I'm ready to resign her.—He's here still! Good morrow, Friend, I cannot leave thee thus dissatisfi'd; what art thou studying on?

FRIENDLY
Love; but it likes me not.

WELLMAN
Why?

FRIENDLY
She is not honest.

WELLMAN
What then? shou'd we hate all that are so, some men wou'd hate their Mothers and their Sisters; a sin against kind.

FRIENDLY
Is it a wise man's part to be in love?

WELLMAN
Let wise men alone; 'twill beseem thee and me well enough.

FRIENDLY
And shall I not commit a sin against friendship?

WELLMAN
What to love where I do? By Heaven, I resign her freely to thee: the creature and I must grow strangers; and by this time she has heard of my designe to marry, and swears and rails, and cries, and curses me. Come, faith I will resign her, and you see Diana will like thee nere the worse for't.

FRIENDLY
I'll but embrace her, hear her speak, and at the most but kiss her.

WELLMAN
Oh heark, he that cou'd live upon the scent of Meat, wou'd live cheaply.

FRIENDLY
I shall never become heartily a man o'th' Town, a kind of flat ungracious Debauchee; an unsufficient dulness reigns about me.

WELLMAN
This Italian breeding has spoil'd thee, and stiffen'd thy behaviour. Come, come, thou shalt to her, and she shall like thee.

FRIENDLY
But if she shou'd not, Friend!

WELLMAN
Fear her not, 'tis her Trade, and what she'as practis'd long with many Lovers.

FRIENDLY
Was she not true to thee?

WELLMAN
I do believe she was, whilst she was mine.

FRIENDLY
Was she a sinner ere you saw her then?

WELLMAN
Oh a very Strumpet! Pardon me truth. Come, have a good heart, and thou shalt possess her, since thou'rt so in love.

FRIENDLY
Death, man, 'tis Destiny, I cannot help it.

WELLMAN
Nay, I hope so. Come, come, she sells but flesh; so that even in the enjoying thou't regain again thy freedom. Go thy ways.

[Exit **FRIENDLY**. Enter **TRICKWELL**.

How now, Raskal! what make you up so early?

TRICKWELL
He that will thrive, must be early stirring, Sir: I am going to get the Peny, Sir; Aye, Heaven has endow'd me with industry, I thank it.

WELLMAN
And what good Acquaintance have you, Sirrah? no handsome women?

TRICKWELL
Faith, Sir, yes, some do start up now and then; but a Pox on't, when they have run through all the Trades and Degrees of the Citie, they pass at the other side of the Town for new Faces, and are caught up by your Courtiers for innocent and honest, though the Citie-Surgeon have had good Customers of 'um; and by my Troth, Sir, I hate to cheat a Gentleman with false Ware. But last night—

WELLMAN

What last night?

TRICKWELL
I was horrid drunk at Supper with one Sir John Empty, a brave young fool for my purpose; I brought him a Wench, one Betty Cogit; a Pox on her, a pretty drunken Whore 'tis, and handsome: if she can serve you, I can bed my Knight with any other.

WELLMAN
Away, you're a Rogue; I'll talk about it another time. Farewel: Have a care of Mr. Dashit, Sirrah.

[Exit **WELLMAN**

TRICKWELL
Let Mr. Dashit have a care of me; I'll take care he shall be cozen'd most plentifully. Now for some new device! what shall it be?

[Enter **JACK**, a boy with Barbers things.

JACK
Pray, Sir, which is the way to Cheapside, to the Sun-Tavern?

TRICKWELL
Sun-Tavern, Childe! what wou'dst thou do there?

JACK
Whe, Sir, I am sent for to trim Mr. Dashit; and tho he be my God-father, I know not the way to his house.

TRICKWELL
Why, art thou a Barber?

JACK
A Barber-Surgeon, Sir.

TRICKWELL
To what Bawdy-house does your Master belong? and what's your name?

JACK
John Scowre, an't like your Worship.

TRICKWELL
John Scowre! Good Mr. John Scowre, I desire your farther acquaintance. Nay, be cover'd, my dainty boy. Is thy Master at home?

JACK
My Father, forsooth, you mean; but he's dead.

TRICKWELL
And laid in's Grave, good boy?

JACK
Yes, Sir, and my Mother keeps shop.

TRICKWELL
A good witty boy; thou't live to read a Chapter to the Family, and write Sermons, John, in time, wo't thou not?

JACK
In grace a God, Sir.

TRICKWELL
And whither art thou going now, John?

JACK
Marry, forsooth, to trim Mr. Dashit the Vintner, He's my Godfather, I told you, forsooth.

TRICKWELL
Good boy, hold up thy head. Prithee do one thing for me; my name's Hazard.

JACK
He! good Mr. Hazard!

[Bows.

TRICKWELL
Lend me thy Barbers Implements.

JACK
Oh Lord, Sir!

TRICKWELL
Well spoken, a fine boy! What are they worth, childe?

JACK
Oh Lord, Sir, worth I know not.

TRICKWELL
A witty childe! Here's a shilling for thee. Where dost live, John?

JACK
At the three Washballs, forsooth, in Mincing-lane.

TRICKWELL
Aye, I know't; a delicate boy! I have an odde Jest in my head, childe, to trim Mr. Dashit: 'Tis for a wager, boy, a humour; I'll return thy things presently. Hold, let's see—

[Takes off his Apron, and takes his things.

JACK
What mean ye, Mr. Hazard?

TRICKWELL
Nothing, child, but a Jest. Go drink a flaggon, and I'll return presently.

JACK
Pray, Sir, do not stay.

TRICKWELL
As I'm an honest man—The three Washbals, John?

JACK
Aye, Sir.

TRICKWELL
Good: And if I do not shave Mr. Dashit, my ingenuity wants an edge. Let me see, a Barber! My villanous tongue will betray me; I must step in and disguise a little. For my speech, what if it be broken French, or a Northern or a Welch Barber? Good, the Widow Scowres man: good, newly hir'd a Journeyman; very well: I have my Cue, and will proceed, happy be luck—

[Exit **TRICKWELL**

SCENE II

SCENE: Changes to Corina's house.

Enter **CORINA** with her Hair loose, raving, and **MR DUNWELL**.

MRS DUNWELL
Nay, dear sweet childe, do not torment thy self thus violently: say Wellman be to be marri'd, are there no more young Gentlemen, no more both handsome and rich? Come, come, you cou'd not expect to build Tabernacles with him.

CORINA
Damn your sententious Nonsence, let me go loose as the winds when mad, when raging mad. 'Twas you, Heaven curse ye for't, that first seduc'd me, swore that he lov'd me, wou'd eternally; and when my Vertue had resolv'd me good, damn'd Witch, whose trade is Lying and Confusion, you hard besieg'd it round with tales of Wellman, repeated all his Charms so often o're, my Heart began to yield, and Vertue fade like flowers with too much heat; which when you saw; a Curse upon your Tongue, you told him where the part was feeblest here—told him my strength, and how he best might conquer: and he, oh lovely Tyrant, found it true, and never ceas'd till he had vanquisht all. Leave me, thou Witch, that hast reduc'd this soul, this body too, to nothing but a Grave.

MRS DUNWELL

To nothing! Marry and that's not my fault; I have made as many proffers of your Virginity since he ruin'd it, as if you had been my own Daughter a thousand times, so I have; but you were so peevish, you ever stood in your own light; nothing wou'd down with you but Wellman.

CORINA
Hell take thy tongue, or blast it.

MRS DUNWELL
Aye, for God forgive me, it has been a thousand times forsworn for you, and yet I've brought you to nothing. Have I not brought you English and French Merchants of the best Rank, Jews of the richest Tribes, Irish Lords, Scottish Earls, and lastly, the Dutch Agent, who offer'd ye a Tun of money? and is all this nothing? Come, come, had you had grace, you had made something of all these; but nothing but Wellman was regarded.

CORINA
Oh that hated Name, like some black Charm it curdles up my bloud.

MRS DUNWELL
And yet, a my conscience the Gentleman's an honest Gentleman, and one you have got fairly by; I hope him to you, and have I this for my labour? Well, Mary Dunwell,—
[Weeps]
—go thy ways; Mary Dunwell, thy kinde heart will bring thee to the Hospital.

CORINA
I'll be reveng'd; nothing but dire Revenge shall satiate my Rage. Methinks I am inspir'd with manly strength, a bloudy courage swells my rising heart, and I shall act some wonderous dismal mischief. And yet to see him bleed, he that has sworn so many tender things, and breath'd 'em all in kisses on my bosome; but now all those, and thousands new invented, he pays another Mistriss more beloved. I die, I die, and cannot bear that thought, by which I finde I'm feeble woman still. Why didst thou? tell me, for I'll here begin, why didst thou praise this Monster?—To my soul.

[Draws a Dagger and takes hold of her.

MRS DUNWELL
Heavens, Madam, hold and hear me: I did praise him, I confess; I said he was a fool, a lavish fool, one that lov'd women more than his Religion, that he kept high, and lov'd most ardently: but what of this? the wind you see is turn'd.

CORINA
Turn all then to confusion; turn, thou Witch, 'tis I will play the Devil. Heart, resolve, and set down this decree, never to rest till thou hast made him equal to me, wretched.

[Enter **BOY**.

BOY
Madam, Mr. Wellman and Mr. Friendly are below, and desire leave to kiss your hand.

CORINA

Oh he's grown ceremonious in his Visits. No more, I will be calm, as if my fortune knew no change; I will dissemble, smile; I'll shew my self all woman in my Art,

[Puts the Dagger and Pistol in her two Pockets.

But be a very Devil in my heart.

[Enter **WELLMAN** and **FRIENDLY**.

WELLMAN
How now Corina, what disorder's this?

CORINA
Oh my dear life! this woman has displeas'd me; but one kinde look from thee chases all other thoughts out of my soul.

WELLMAN
But what's the matter? do not dissemble with me.

CORINA
With thee! far be such art from thy Corina's tongue; you've taught her truth with love. What else shou'd such a Master teach a Mistriss? Come, I forgive her now: Alas, she'as lost the little Dog you gave me. Wou'd it not grieve one to loose ought of thine?

WELLMAN
Fie, fie, cry for a Dog! what wou'dst thou do for me that pay'st such tributes to a poor worthless Animal?

CORINA [Aside]
For thee, weep tears of bloud; but 'tis impossible I cou'd be robb'd of thee by ought but death. I know thy noble heart—to be a Traytor.

WELLMAN
Thou art so fond, thou mind'st nothing but me; sees thou not my friend?

CORINA
Yes, and love him too, next to thy self, by Heaven; for he's as great a Villain, being he's man. Come, Sir, you must not be so sad; I'll sing and dance, do any thing to make you gay and smile: for trust me, Sir, I hate sad Company. Heavens, what ails you, Sir? have you the Tooth-ach, Sir? I've many remedies for that.

FRIENDLY
No, my pain is at my heart; have you a Cure for that?

CORINA
A thousand. Kinde Eyes, soft Sighs and Kisses well appli'd.

FRIENDLY
'Twill but increase the pain: 'twas so I caught it.

CORINA
Alas, I'll sing then; I have a thousand Songs, so pretty and so loving.—

FRIENDLY
Still that but hurts me more.

CORINA
Then I've no Remedies.
[Sighs]
Hah, what Ring is that? I like it, and must have it.

WELLMAN
No you must not, Love.

CORINA
Fie, you call me Love, and cry I must not! I say I will. How now, who is't commands where I am?

WELLMAN
You intirely; but this Ring I cannot part with.

CORINA
'Tis my Rivals: Rot with his finger, how it fires my bloud, and the red flame kindles about my face, and will betray my heart! Come, 'tis a trifle.

WELLMAN
I care not for the value.

CORINA
Has it a worth besides its own intrinsick one?

WELLMAN
Nay, you're of late so peevish and so jealous, that you grow troublesome.

CORINA
Jealous! by this dear mouth not I.

[Kisses him.

Come, give me the Ring; by all that's kinde, you shall: By all our Loves, and by all those soft Embraces when in my Arms you swore eternal Love, eternal Faith, I do conjure ye give it me: I never us'd to beg such Toys in vain.

WELLMAN
Thou art uncivilly importunate. Go, fool, thou sha't not ha't; I care not for thee nor thy Jealousie.

CORINA

He speaks his soul in that, which from his mouth destroys all my dissembling. I know that Ring, thou falser than the Devil; I know it is Marinda's, your new Mistriss: take her, but take her far from me be sure; keep her as thou wou'dst secrets that wou'd damn thee; for if she take but Air, she is no more; it will be all infected with my Sighs and Curses, and 'twill be catching, Sir: look to't, it will.

WELLMAN
Thou'rt grown a hectoring Whore!

CORINA
Leave me, or such another word from thee will put thee into danger. Dar'st thou upbraid the faults thou hast created? Furies possess me, that I may incounter the like Fate or killing Blasts! Oh I cou'd rave to think I want that power that might destroy thee!

WELLMAN
Do not turn Witch before thy time, Corina.

CORINA [Sighing]
I wou'd I were, that I might be an age in damning thee: But words are Air that blow above thy head, and cannot wound nor blast.

WELLMAN
Nay, if you rave, I'll leave ye; fare ye well.—You will not go.

[She catches him.

CORINA
And is it true, hast thou abandon'd me? Canst thou forget our numerous Blisses past, the hours we've wasted out in Tales of Love, and curst all interruption but of Kisses, which 'twixt thy charming words I ever gave thee; when the whole live-long day we thought too short, yet blest the coming night? Hast thou forgot, false are thy Vows, all perjur'd, and thy Faith broken as my poor lost forsaken heart? and wou'dst thou wish me live to see this Change! Cou'dst thou believe, if thou hadst hid it from the talking world, my heart cou'd not have found it out by sympathie! A foolish unconsidering faithless man!

WELLMAN
This is as troublesome as Rage to me.

[Breaks from her.

CORINA
Some comfort that thou dost confess thou'rt base; and this last blaze of my departing Love, has but a minutes light, and now 'tis gone.

WELLMAN
It went in fume, and leaves a scent behinde it which does offend my sense: Farewel.

[Goes out.

CORINA

Farewel. And dost thou think I'll part with thee thus tamely! Faithless unthinking fool, by Heaven, no other woman shall possess thee; the perjur'd heart you gave, thus I demand:

[Takes a Pistol out of her pocket, fires it at his breast; it only flashes in the pan: **FRIENDLY** runs to her; she throws it away.]

Oh damn this treacherous instrument, false as the heart 'twas aim'd at: But since, like Coward States, I wanted courage to attack the Foe, I'll turn my Fury into civil Broyls, and hurl all to confusion here within.

[Offers to stab her self; **FRIENDLY** runs to her, prevents her, and she seems fainted a little while in his arms.

FRIENDLY
Pray leave her, Sir, your presence but inflames her.

WELLMAN
I will: look to her, prithee. I was too rash, and mist from too much violence and rage—I might have more securely done the business.
[Aside]
Pray leave me, Sir, I cannot go, a fire in my blood confines me here:
'Tis not a vertuous flame!
No, raging Lust my wilful fate does move;
The Gods themselves cannot be wise and love.

CORINA [Aside]
This man whom I abhor because his Friend, through all my rage, I see has passion for me, raise it, ye Powers, till it become so high to be employ'd to any use, I'll put it to a fatal instrument of my Revenge.

FRIENDLY
Loveliest of all your injur'd Sex.—

CORINA
You're charitable to the forsaken, Sir, but 'tis alas all thrown away on me; for I can never more believe there can be honesty in man, since Wellman is all Vice.

FRIENDLY
What Devil, envious of his glorious Choice, contriv'd to make him faithless to such Beauty! Had I that Blessing, which I dare not name, hardly dare wish, 'tis so above my merit, I shou'd dispise, as useless and unnecessary, all the vast Joys besides Heaven has in store, and at thy feet lay all my Fortunes down, and set up my eternal rest with thee.

CORINA
Just so he spoke, and I fond fool believ'd, and tir'd him out with love; but you're all false, inconstant, faithless Tyrants, and betrayers even in that very minute that you gain us; we forfeit all our hopes in you for ever. I can believe no more.

FRIENDLY

Silence and Modestie were wont to be my two accustom'd Vertues; but my Love grows high and rages in me like a storm: Wou'd you'd believe my Vows; but you have been deceiv'd that way alreadie: therefore, thou dear, thou lovely injur'd fair one, credit my plain Synceritie. I love, and to be short, wou'd have thee pay my flame, I will be grateful in what way you please. Take me to your Embraces, to your Bed. I am not us'd to ask such Questions, Madam, and want terms fit to dress 'em in.

CORINA
And do you take me then for such a Creature, that have no sense but Appetite, the Brutal part of Love? Forbear to name it to me, you offend me.

FRIENDLY
Forgive me; I wou'd have you love me too: and if I have too hastily run o're what ought to have been said of my vast Passion, and came too rudely on the wisht-for part, 'tis the effects of youthful ignorance, of hot desire, and eager to be happy.

CORINA
How shall I fain to yield!
[Aside]
There's such a seeming honest plainness, Sir, in what you say, in spight of all my grief, I listen to your Language. Cou'd you be true, cou'd you convince me throughly that you lov'd!

FRIENDLY [Kneeling]
What Art will do't? what Vows, what Protestations, what Proofs, what Gifts, besides a faithful Heart?

CORINA
Shall I, or can I trust again? Oh fool, how natural 'tis for women to believe! But when you've gain'd the utmost that you ask, will you not then grow cold?

FRIENDLY
As soon the Sun shall lose its native heat, denying warmth to Flowers.

CORINA
I must have more than this: Can you believe this heart that has been us'd so ill already, can you trust on feeble Vows? Can you be bravely kinde, resolve a Deed wou'd shake a Soul that is not fixt in Love?

FRIENDLY
Is it a Deed that I may do with honour?

CORINA
I did not studie that; but if there be any thing that stands in competition with your Love, it is not worth my owning.

FRIENDLY
Be it what it will, 'tis for so rich a Prize, without demanding what, I'll vow it done.

CORINA
I hate this Wellman: You may guess the rest. Good day to you.

FRIENDLY
Leaving me! by Heaven we must not part: Love and Desire are madly raving in me; my impatient Heat admits of no resistance: I cannot live, without you grant me instantly that which I dare not ask.

[Follows on his knees.

CORINA
As long as Wellman lives, I've made a Vow never to love again; yet am I understood.

FRIENDLY
Will you be mine when Wellman is no more?

CORINA
By all my hopes, by my last best of wishes.

FRIENDLY
Be mine, and onely mine, for ever mine?

CORINA
Inviolably yours.

FRIENDLY
Then hear me, on my knees I make this Vow: Wellman shall die before to morrows light. Now may I hope my Bliss?

CORINA
Yes, when the Deed is done. And for a Token that you have dispatcht him, bring me that Diamond that he wears, and which he did refuse me.—Do you pawse—

FRIENDLY
Onely the manner, Sweet—

CORINA
Oh you may pick a sudden Quarrel with him, word it to blows, and then take all advantages.

FRIENDLY
And will my Vows to kill him, merit nothing?

CORINA
No, I have vow'd, and if you love, you'l yield to't.

FRIENDLY
Enough: Farewel.

[She goes out.

Delays in Love's the Lovers onely Hell.

[Going out hastily stops.

Hah! whither wou'd my hastie steps misguide me! was I not rushing on to kill a Friend? to kill a Friend, oh 'tis to kill my self! Passion, how hellish art thou? oh how vile, to kill a Friend to gain a sinful woman for Appetite, for sensual end, and momentarie pleasure;
And Vices like to swelling Rivers flow,
The further that they run they bigger grow.
Heaven! how neer was I to being undone!
I'll flie, lest the temptation overtake me.

[Exit.

SCENE III

SCENE: Changes to Dashit's house.

Enter **MRS DASHET** with a bag of money, **MR DASHET** following.

MR DASHET
Well, is the money right?

MRS DASHET
Just fiftie pound, Honey, in good hard Half-crowns.

MR DASHET
Well, Mr. Trickwell, 'tis your confounded Worship puts me to this Charge; but an I catch thee, an I do not charge thee with as many Irons, mayst thou cozen me again, Knave, mayst thou cozen me again. Well, Wife, is the Barber come? I'll be trim'd, and then to my Neighbour Glistens the Goldsmith to new furnish my self with Plate.

MRS DASHET
Truely Husband, surely Heaven is not pleas'd with our Vocation; we wink at the sins of our Customers, our Wines are meerly Protestant, and I now speak it with grief of heart, we frie Fish with salt Butter, to the burthen of my Conscience, calling our Wines by fortie heathenish names to disguise truth.

MR DASHET
Hold your prating; a Pox of your Conscience, go minde your business in the Bar, score double, and mend the matter with a vengeance.

[Exit **MRS DASHET** lays the money on the Table.

[Enter **TRICKWELL** drest like a Barber.

How now, Friend, what are you?

TRICKWELL

A Barber, Sir, the Widow Scowres man, an't like your Worship; my name's Timothy Hazard, Sir.

MR DASHET
Very well, very well; and how does my Godson, Timothy?

[**MR DASHET** sits down in a Chair, he puts the things about him.

TRICKWELL
Very well, an't like your Worship; he's gone to trim Parson Cuffett.

MR DASHET
And how long have you been a Barber, Timothy?

TRICKWELL
A Year, an't like your Worship, come Christmas.

MR DASHET
What, what, and a good Workman, Timothy? And may I trust my self in thy hands, Timothy?

TRICKWELL
Oh doubt me not, Sir, I'll shave your Worship as cleverly, as your Worship shall confess, by that time I've done.—Hah, 'tis Cash!

[Feels the Money-bag. Whilst he is washing him they talk.

MR DASHET
Well, Timothy, and what's the News, Timothy? You Barbers are notable News-mongers, good Commonwealthsmen: You—

TRICKWELL
Marrie, Sir, I know none but of the Speaking Childe and the Monster.

MR DASHET
How, the Monsters! what Monster, good Timothy?

TRICKWELL
Has not your Worship heard of the Monster, the Gravesend -Monster?

MR DASHET
By my Troth not I.

TRICKWELL
Why, Sir, there came ashore last night four and twentie huge horrible monsterous devouring—

MR DASHET
Bless us! what?

TRICKWELL

Whales, Sir; which no sooner came ashore, but they turn'd into fearful Elephants that roar'd, then into Cockatrices that crow'd and frighted all the Judges out of Westminster hall.

MR DASHET
Good Lord!

TRICKWELL
And in a moment these Cockatrices were turn'd into so many huge Giants in Scarlet, with Triple Crowns on their heads, and forked Tongues that hiss so loud, the noise is heard to the Royal Exchange; which has put the Citizens into such a Consternation, that 'tis thought the world's at an end.

MR DASHET
Good Lord! And what may this portend, Timothy?

TRICKWELL
Portend, Sir, Poperie, Sir, Poperie; and these Monsters are call'd the four and twentie Whores of Babylon.

MR DASHET
Oh monsterous! Four and twentie Whores! the Nation will be over-run with Poperie indeed, Timothy.: Bless us, what monsterous things are these Popish Monsters! Well, in grace of God my Wife and I will go see these four and twentie Whores. Nay, nay, God bless little England; this must portend right down Poperie, that's certain. Well, and hast thou no merrie News, Timothy?

TRICKWELL
Faith, Sir, they say that there's five and twentie couple of Bears are to dance a Dance in Paris-Garden before the King; and four and twentie couple of French Apes play to 'em upon Flute doux.

MR DASHET
Oh Pox, Timothy, this must be a lye,
Timothy; and this be not a lye,
I am an Ass efaith: Four and twentie
Bears dance to Flutes douxes! Ha, ha, ha.

TRICKWELL
'Tis credible reported, Sir.—Shut your Eyes close, Sir, closer yet, Sir, this Ball will make 'em smart.

MR DASHET
Aye, aye, Timothy, I do wink.

TRICKWELL
Hold, Sir, your head will take cold;

[Puts on a fools cap.

I'll put on your good Worships Night-cap. So, now I'll shave you, Sir. This must along with me, this Beaver too, and now adieu, worshipful Mr. Dashit.

[Leaves him in the Suds, the Bason in's hand, and runs away with the money. Exit.

MR DASHET
Ha, ha, ha! Four and twentie couple of English Bears dance to the Musick of French Apes! Ha, ha, ha! in faith, good Timothy, thou makest my Worship smile,—But heark ye, Timothy, dost know one Trickwell? a villanous Rogue, Timothy, cheated me last night of Fiftie pound in Plate; but I'll Plate him, with a Pox, an I catch him. Come, haste, good Timothy. Art thou free, Timothy? I am one of the Common Council, Timothy, and may do thee good shortly. Why Timothy! Timothy! dost leave me in the Suds? Why Timothy! I shall be blinde with winking.

[Wipes his Eyes.

Timothy! Hah, you—Wife, my money, Wife!

[Enter **MRS DASHET**.

MRS DASHET
What's the noise here? you are always bawling.

MR DASHET
'Owns, ye Whore, where's Timothy?

MRS DASHET
What Timothy?

MR DASHET
Why the Barber, Jade, the Barber.

MRS DASHET
The Barber! I saw him go half a quarter of an hour since. Why, are you not trim'd?

MR DASHET
Trim'd, a Pox trim ye; where's the money, the money, the money, ye Jade? I am trim'd with a vengeance!

MRS DASHET
What's the money gone! the whole Fiftie pound in the bag!

MR DASHET
I have wink'd fair, in the Devils name.

[Enter **JACK**. Kneels.

JACK
Pray, Godfather, give me your Blessing.

MR DASHET
A Pox of Blessing, I am Cursing, Rogue: where's Timothy, thy Mothers man Timothy?

JACK
My Mother has no such, forsooth.

MR DASHET
My money! my fiftie pound! A Plague of all Timothies; who was't trim'd me?

JACK
I know not, Godfather; onely one met me and borrow'd my Furniture, for a Jest, he said.

MR DASHET
What kind of Fellow was't? Oh—

JACK
A little slender nimble well-spoken fellow, Sir.

MR DASHET
Oh 'tis Trickwell, that Rogue Trickwell! a black Hair and Eye-brows, and grey Eyes?

JACK
Yes, Godfather.

MR DASHET
Aye, aye, 'tis he. Raise the street upon him; I'll hang him if there be Law for money. Oh I shall faint! Wife, wife, fetch me the Rosa solus.

MRS DASHET
Good Husband, take comfort in the Lord, I'll play the Devil but I'll recover it; have a good heart, 'tis but a weeks false scoring in the Parliament-time.

[Fetches the bottle, he drinks.

MR DASHET
So, some comfort: Wife, whe Wife, I say, is there any Musick in the house?

MRS DASHET
Yes, Sweet-heart, Mr. Squeeks Noyse.

MR DASHET
Bid 'em play then: And John come kiss me now, now, now, and John come kiss me now.
[Sings]
Bid 'em play; laugh thou and be merrie, for I'll go dance, cast up my Accounts, and hang my self presently. I will not curse, but a Pox on Trickwell, he has shav'd me, he has trim'd me! I will go hang my self; but first let's have a Dance.

[Exeunt dancing with the bottle in's hand, and sings, John come kiss me, &c.

ACT THE THIRD

SCENE the First

Enter **MARINDA**, **DIANA**, **AMPLE**.

MARINDA
Come, prithee Ample, sing the Song Wellman made upon the Kiss I gave him.

DIANA
No, prithee don't, my stomack turns against kissing extreamly.

MARINDA
Why, Diana?

DIANA
By the faith I have in this Beautie, 'tis the most unsavorie Ceremonie, the most sawcie Custom to Ladies; every Fellow now-a-daies with greasie sweatie Faces, stinking Breath, and nastie Teeth, must take a bodie over the Lips with such familiaritie; nay they think 'tis grateful to us too. Lord, there was an old Judge laid me over the face last night, and did so squeeze his grizly Brissles through my Lips, I'd as live a kist a row of Pins with the points to me; and yet I was forc'd to take it, take it with a Curtsie too: for my part I had as lieve they should belch in my face.

MARINDA
Fie, what a Comparison's there!

DIANA
Sutable to the beastly Complement; and yet I love kissing too, if I may chuse my man and place.

MARINDA
Fie, if any one shou'd hear ye!

DIANA
Let a thousand, I'd not be asham'd; 'tis not those that talk roguishly, that are to be suspected: you shall have a hypocritical holy Sister mince that publickly, that she'll receive with open arms privately: For my own part, I consider Nature without Apparel, without disguising; I give thoughts, words, and truth, a modest boldness; I love no prohibited things, and I wou'd have nothing prohibited but by Vertue.

MARINDA
But we must consider the world, who thinks severe modestie a womans Vertue.

DIANA
Fie, fie, Vertue is freedom, handsome, cheerful mirth; I hate a severe, froward, ignorant, ill-bred behaviour in a woman; 'tis uncivil, hang't, I'll have none on't. Ample, what think you?

AMPLE
Faith, Madam, I can onely stand up for Kissing; I never ventur'd farther, tho I wou'd fain.

DIANA
Thou art not of my minde; for I'll nere marrie.

AMPLE
Marrie God forbid! what will you do then?

DIANA
Ene strive against the flesh: Marrie! no, faith, Husbands are like Lots in a book, one may prick a hundred times and finde all blanks. A Husband! a Hangman: a careless domineering insolent thing, that grows like Corral, whilst under water, soft and tender; but married, and above the waves, hard, stubborn, not to be bow'd nor manag'd: whilst your humble servant, Oh how assiduous, troublesomely officious and busie; but wed, the worstbred Tyrant and Sloven in nature. No, no, I'll live my own woman, I—and let the worst come to the worst, I had rather be call'd Wanton than a Fool.

MARINDA
Oh but a vertuous Marriage!

DIANA
Vertuous Marriage! there's no more affinitie between Vertue and Marriage, than a man and his Horse: Wedlock may manage Vertue in the right way, but 'tis oftner loose and unbridled. I hate restraint upon my Vertue, or to owe it to the honour of a Husband; yet I like thy match well enough, a handsome man, good humour, wittie, and wilde; but my Sir John is such a tool, fit to make nothing but a Cuckold of. See if they be not here.

[Enter **SIR JOHN EMPTIE** and **WELLMAN**.

WELLMAN
My sweet Marinda!

SIR JOHN
Good morrow, my little Sooterkin; how is't, my prettie Life?—Nay, I call all my Mistrisses so.

DIANA
Indeed! How many Mistrisses have you had?

SIR JOHN
Some Nine, or thereabouts.

DIANA
Then you have had nine lives, like a Cat.

SIR JOHN
Mew—you wou'd be kist for that.

DIANA
Yes, if I lik'd the mouth that offer'd it.

SIR JOHN
By my troth, that must not be mine; I do not love to endanger my back with stooping so low: if you wou'd wear Chipeeners, much might be done.—Nay, let me alone to finde a Rowland for your Oliver.

DIANA
Your pestilent wit will never make me asham'd of my shortness: the faults I can mend my self, I blush at; but those which Nature made, let her bear the shame for me, I have nothing to do with it; but you never forget to be wittie on my Beautie, Sir Knight, I shall be even with you.

SIR JOHN
Nor remember, by my troth, but as I do Religion, for Controversie sake onely, no hurt.

DIANA
But, Brother, for I'll now call you so, since my Father this night resolves to contract you—Shall we not have Fiddles and dance? Sir John I'm sure will make one, and my Citie Lover the Aldermans son, Mr. Shatter, he's a most spruce Dancer of the first bench in the School, I'll promise ye.

SIR JOHN
Fore Gad, and well remember'd, he borrow'd a Diamond-Ring of me last night to make a Visit in to a Ladie; and was't you? The Devil take me, an I had thought that, he shou'd nere a had it. Adsbud he's here!

[Enter **MR SHATTER**.

MR SHATTER
Good day to my fair Mistriss.

DIANA
Good morrow, sweet Mr. Shatter.

SIR JOHN
Sweet Mr. Shatter! Pox on him, is he a Rival now?

DIANA
You're fine to day, rich in Jems, Mr. Shatter.

MR SHATTER
A Toy, Madam, I bought to please my finger.

DIANA
I am more pretious to you than your finger; why not to oblige me? Come, I'm no profess'd beggar, you know.

MR SHATTER
Faith and troth, Madam, as I hope to be sav'd—Oh Lord, as the saying is—I protest upon my honour.

DIANA
Do not pawn it for such a trifle.

MR SHATTER
As I'm a Gentleman, as God shall fa'me, I'll give a—

DIANA
Is this yours to give?

MR SHATTER
Oh Lord, Madam, that's such a thing now, why shou'd your Ladyship—you're the strangest Joker, I protest.—

DIANA
Hum! now I remember, I think I have seen this on a persons hand, an humble servant of mine, one Sir John Empty.

MR SHATTER
Pox of her memorie! a such another Madam. Whe, what a Devil's he to her now?

DIANA
Nay, I'm sure this is it.

MR SHATTER
Troth, 'tis, Madam: the poor fellow wanted a little money to treat some women last night, and so he pawn'd it to me. 'Tis a Pawn, good faith, or else you shou'd have it.

SIR JOHN
Heark ye, thou base lying son of a cheating Cit, how dares thy impudence hope to prosper? Were it not for the respect I bear this noble Companie, I wou'd so bang thee!—

[Pulls him aside.

DIANA
How now, what's the matter here?

MR SHATTER
Nothing, Madam, nothing. He was a little uncivil with me last night; for which, because I shou'd not call him to an account, he desir'd to make me any satisfaction. The Coward trembles at my very presence; but I have him on the hip, I'll take the forfeit of his Ring.

SIR JOHN
Heark ye, Sir, what's that you whisper to her?

[Pulls him aside.

MR SHATTER
Nothing, Sir, but to satisfie her that the Ring was yours, not pawn'd to me, but lent to grace my finger; and so I told her I begg'd your pardon for being a little too familiar with your Reputation.

DIANA
Yes indeed, he did; and said you wou'd make him any satisfaction for a rudeness you did him last night, but he wou'd take the forfeit of the Ring for't.

SIR JOHN
How now, ye base Scoundrel!

[Takes him roughly.

MR SHATTER
Hold, hold, my Mistriss does but rally, faith.

DIANA
Thy Mistriss! I disown thee; thou'rt a childe, I'll give thee to my woman. Come, Sister, let's make us ready for the Ball anon. Come, you shall be friends.

SIR JOHN
He shall renounce you then, and restore my Ring; Adsbud he shall.

MR SHATTER
With all my heart, to do you service, Sir.

[Gives him the Ring.

SIR JOHN
And here I make an offer of it.

DIANA
Well, I'll take it, Sir, to make me thine to night. Farewel, Brother, till anon.

[Exit **MARINDA, DIANA, SIR JOHN,** & **AMPLE**.

WELLMAN
To be huft thus by a Coward, a beaten Coward, what madness has possest thee?

MR SHATTER
Aye, but how the Devil did I know he was a Coward? cou'd not you have whisper'd me that?

WELLMAN
Well, Sir, I'll try to make your peace with Diana. Leave me, I've business now.

[Exit **MR SHATTER** Enter **FRIENDLY**.

How now, my friend! what news from Love? is the Ladie of sin kinde? prithee say how; in faith I'll not be angrie.

FRIENDLY

Oh, Wellman! no Age did ere produce so damn'd a Creature so fair, and yet so false: had I been vicious, what a desperate wretched thing I'd been!

WELLMAN
Prithee what's the matter?

FRIENDLY
Heaven! I have been tempted to thy death.

WELLMAN
What is the Furie mad?

FRIENDLY
Most damnable!

WELLMAN
Hearing I'm to be marri'd.

FRIENDLY
She rav'd at first like winds let loose to ruine,
But fixt on this resolve, she calm'd again,
And listen'd to my love, my eager love; which when it urg'd her to create me happie, she prest me to this Murder, as the way, the onely means to gain her heart for ever. Mad with my flame, I cou'd deny her nothing, and then my lawless lust, not I, protested, confirm'd it with a thousand Oaths to kill ye, and bring this Ring to witness you were dead; and then her lovely bodie was my hire.

WELLMAN
Horrid! nothing's defam'd but by its proper self: Physicians abuse Remedies, Lawyers spoil Law, and woman onely is a shame to woman. You've vow'd to kill me?

FRIENDLY
Most solemnly; for, friend, I must enjoy her. Oh that a man of sense shou'd fancie pleasure in one whose soul's so black and infamous; but 'tis my fate, and I must bow before it.

WELLMAN
Thou shalt; I will contrive the means to satisfie thee. Come, I give a Ball to night to my Marinda; thou shalt be there: and by the way, I'll tell thee what we will do to make a seeming Quarrel, that all the world, as well as this Corina, may think I'm kill'd indeed, whilst I, lodg'd in some place obscure, may give thee time to cool this feavourish blood. Shew her this Ring, protest me surely dead; and when thou'rt satiated, we'll laugh at follie. Come, let us go.

[Exeunt.

SCENE II

SCENE: Changes to the street, a shop-door.

Enter **MR GLISTEN** and **MR DASHET**, with a great silver Bason or Punchbowl. Enter **TRICKWELL** in the habit of a Pedler with a box with Trinkets before him. **JERVICE**.

MR DASHET
Well, Neighbour Glisten, I am beholden to you for this credit till next week, and I am pleased in my choice of this piece of Flate; a Punch-bowl is a most fashonable thing, now French Wines are prohibited: I know 'twill please my Wife. Well, I am fortie pound indebted to you for't, honest Mr. Glisten.

MR GLISTEN
Your word's sufficient, Sir, an 'twere for a thousand pound.

MR DASHET
A Pox of the Rogue that robb'd me! Well, I shall catch him; and if I do, he shall half rot in Fetters in the Dungeon till he despair; then I'll hire a Parson on purpose that shall perswade him he is damn'd; then after see him with my own eyes hang'd without singing any Psalm: Lord, Lord, that he shou'd have but one neck!

MR GLISTEN
Oh, Neighbour, you must use a Conscience in all things; but do your will. You'll command me no farther?

MR DASHET
No, onely lend me your servant to carrie this Bowl home to my Peg; I am to step into Leaden-hall.

MR GLISTEN
Willingly, Sir: Here, Jervice, carrie home this Plate.

MR DASHET
To my Wives own hands deliver it, good Jervice.

JERVICE
I'll warrant you, Sir.

MR DASHET
To her own hand, honest Jervice.

JERVICE
I have deliver'd better things than this to a womans own hand, Sir, before now.

[Exit **JERVICE** with the Bowl, and **MR GLISTEN** in.

TRICKWELL
Monsieur, please you to buy a very fine delicate Ball, a sweet Ball, a Camphere-ball.

MR DASHET
Prithee away.

TRICKWELL

One a Ball to shave, one a Ball to scowre.

MR DASHET
Name 'em not to me, talk not of shaving; a Pox of the Rogue, I have been shav'd, I have.

[Exit **MR DASHET**.

TRICKWELL
I'll shave ye smoother yet: That Bowl, that delicious Bowl, I must be drunk out of; I have a fancie for't, it is too good for cheating Vintners: I say it must be mine; therefore, my worshipful Dashit, look to't: What tho there be rounds in a Ladder, and knots in a Halter? hang the Devil, I'll do't; I must draw a Lot for the great Punch-bowl.

[Goes out.

SCENE III

SCENE: Changes to Mr. Dashit's house.

Enter **MRS DASHET** and **JERVICE** with the Bowl.

MRS DASHET
Nay, Jervice, stay and drink, good Jervice; and how does Mrs. Glisten? I knew her well, she was a very good patient Creature, efaith; she has born, and born, and bore again, good woman, as well as I, with a bad Husband; yet I can finde no fault in Mr. Glisten: Here's to him, Jervice, he knew me before I was married; an honest man he is,—

[Drinks.

—and a thriftie, I'll warrant him; and his Wife's a proper woman as any in Cheapside.

JERVICE
Yes, indeed forsooth, so she is.

MRS DASHET
She paints now, and yet she keeps her Husband's Customers still. Introth, Jervice, a handsome Wife in a fine carv'd seat, is the best Ware in a mans shop.

JERVICE
Yes, indeed forsooth, so 'tis.

MRS DASHET
But well, Jervice, remember me to your Master and Mistriss, and tell 'em I acknowledge the receipt of this, acknowledge the receipt.—This 'tis to have good Education, and to be brought up in a Tavern; and though my Husband be a Citizen, all London knows I keep as good Companie as any she within the Walls. Good day, honest Jervice.

[Exit **JERVICE**.

[Enter **TRICKWELL** drest like a Prentise, with a Jole of Salmon.

TRICKWELL
Fair hour to you, Mistriss.

MRS DASHET
A prettie Complement! I'll write it down: A beautiful thought to you, Sir.

TRICKWELL
Your Husband and my Master Mr. Glisten has sent you a Jole of fresh Salmon, and they intend to come both to Dinner presently to season your new Bowl, forsooth, which your Husband intreats you wou'd send back by me, that his Arms may be engraven on it, which he forgot before.

MRS DASHET
Are you sent by no Token? Nay, I have a wit.

TRICKWELL
Yes forsooth, by the same Token he was dry shav'd this morning.

MRS DASHET
A sad Token, but true: here, pray commend me to your Master and Mistriss, and tell 'em I expect 'em impatiently.

[Gives him the Bowl, takes the Salmon. Exit **TRICKWELL**.

Impatient was well again! Sam! why Sam, I say!

SAM
Anon, anon, forsooth.

MRS DASHET
Come quickly, spread the Table, lay Napkins, and do ye hear? perfume the Room a little; it does so smell of this prophane Tobacco! I could never endure this ungodly Tobacco, since our Doctor told me 'twas a bane to Propagation.—So spread handsomly: Lord, these Boys do things so arsie-versie! You shew your breeding. Well, I am a Gentlewoman by my Sisters side, I can tell you: so—methodically. Hum! I wonder where I got that word! Oh 'twas Sir John Empty bid me kiss him methodically; 'tis a sweet man!

[Enter **MR DASHET**.

MR DASHET
Well, Tony Dashit, be not discourag'd, be not disheartned, thou wilt recover all.

MRS DASHET
Oh are you come, Husband? where are they?

MR DASHET
How now! how now! how now! what, a Feast towards! and in my private Parlour! Who treats, who treats, Peg?

MRS DASHET
Prithee leave fooling; are they come?

MR DASHET
Come! who come?

MRS DASHET
Lord, How strange you make it!

MR DASHET
Strange! what's strange? is the woman mad!

MRS DASHET
Aye strange: You know of none that sent me a Jole of Salmon, you—and said they wou'd come dine with me!

MR DASHET
Hah, fresh Salmon! peace, not I; peace, the Messenger has mistaken the house: let's eat it up quickly, before it be inquir'd for. Come, come, Vineger quickly, Sam—Some good luck yet, efaith; I never tasted Salmon that relisht better in my life. Well, 'tis a rare thing to feed at other mens cost.

MRS DASHET
Other mens cost! prithee did not you send this Salmon?

MR DASHET
No, I say, no.

MRS DASHET
By Mr. Glisten's man?

MR DASHET
I say no.

MRS DASHET
Who sent word that he and his Wife wou'd come to dinner with me?

MR DASHET
No, no.

[He eats like mad all this while.

MRS DASHET
And hancel my new Bowl.

[He lays down his knife and starts.

MR DASHET
Hah, Bowl!

MRS DASHET
And withal, commanded me to send the Bowl back.

MR DASHET
Hah, back!

MRS DASHET
That your Arms might be put on't.

MR DASHET
Oh!

MRS DASHET
By the same token that you were dry shaven this morning.

MR DASHET
Oh!

MRS DASHET
And thereupon I sent back the Bowl: nay and I bear not a brain—

MR DASHET
And is the Bowl gone? is it deliver'd? departed? defunct? hah!

MRS DASHET
Delivered? yes sure, 'tis delivered.

MR DASHET
I will never more say my Prayers; and is the Bowl gone?

MRS DASHET
Gone: God is my witness I deliver'd it with no more designe to be cozen'd on't, than the childe unborn.

MR DASHET
Look to my house, I am haunted with Evil Spirits: hear me, thou Plague to man, thou Wife thou, if I have not my Bowl again, I will go to the Devil; I'll to a Conjurer: look to my house, I'll raise all the Wise men in London.

[Exit in rage.

MRS DASHET
Bless me, what fearful words are these! I trust in God he is but drunk sure.

[Enter **TRICKWELL** as before.

TRICKWELL
I must have my Salmon, I cannot afford the old Rogue so good a bit; I must have it to season my Punch. Now for a Master-piece: Fair Mistriss—

MRS DASHET
Oh have I caught ye! Sam, shut up the doors, Sam.

TRICKWELL
Peace, good Mistress, I'll tell you all: A Jest, a meer Jest; your Husband did it onely to fright ye: the Bowl's at my Masters, and thither your Husband's gone, and has sent me in all haste, lest you shou'd be over-frighted, to invite you to come to dinner to him.

MRS DASHET
Praise Heaven 'tis no worse!

TRICKWELL
And bad me desire you to send the Salmon before, and your self to follow: My Mistriss will be very glad to see you.

MRS DASHET
I pray take it. Well, I was never so out of my wits in my life: Pray thank your Mistriss.

[Exit **TRICKWELL** with the Salmon.

How my heart beats still, beshrew him! Sam, my Hood, Sam, and Gloves, and Scarf, quickly.

[Enter **MR DASHET**.

MR DASHET
How now, whither are you janting, hah?

MRS DASHET
Come, play the fool no longer, will you go?

MR DASHET
Whither, in the name of Madness, whither?

MRS DASHET
Whither! why to Mr. Glisten's to eat the Salmon. How strange you make it!

MR DASHET
Your meaning, Jade, your meaning.

MRS DASHET
Lord bless me, did not you send for me and for the Salmon, by the self-same fellow that came for the Bowl?

MR DASHET
'Tis well, 'tis wonderous well! and are you in your fight wits, Jade, are you?

MRS DASHET
An you make an Ass of me, I'll make an Ox of you, I tell ye that.

MR DASHET
Nay, Jade, be patient; for look ye, I may be mad, or drunk, or so; tho you can bear more than I, I do well: I will not curse; but Heaven knows my minde. Come, let's go hear some Musick. I will never pray again, that's certain: Let's go hear some doleful Musick. Nay, if Heaven forget to prosper Knaves, the Citie's like to thrive: I'll go hang my self out of the way.

ACT THE FOURTH

SCENE the First

Enter **SIR LYONELL**, Mr. Wellman, Friendly, Sir John Emptie, Mr. Shatter, Marinda, Diana, Petronella, and other women and men; with Musick.

SIR LYONELL
More Lights there, Boy, more Wine and Lights.— Come, come, son Wellman, for so I must call you now; introth you are not merrie, Sir, not heartily merrie: Come, we'll have tother Dance, efact we will, Mr. Wellman. Diana, whe Girl, I say! Adsme you're all out of sorts; I thought thy Tongue and heels cou'd never have been idle: Come, come, hands, hands, for shame.

SIR JOHN
Come, Mrs. Diana, I'm your man at this sport; I never stand out at these businesses: Your hand, fair Mistriss.

[Snatches her hand.

FRIENDLY
You lie, Sir.

SIR JOHN
Do I, Sir? I vow to God, I ask your pardon, Sir; I durst to have sworn I'd been in the right.

DIANA
What, quarrelling about the Spoil before the Victorie!

SIR JOHN
Nay, Madam, as for that matter, I'm a man of Reason, and Frank Friendly's an honest fellow, and my friend.

FRIENDLY

You lie again, Sir.

SIR JOHN
Well, well, Sir, you are dispos'd to be merrie, or so, but there be more Ladies—Whe, what the Devil ails he, tro?

MR SHATTER
Pox on't, how rarely he huffs now! Well, it's a most admirable thing this same Courage, if a man had but the knack on't!

SIR LYONELL
Come, Zouks, you're tardie, villanous: Young Men and Maids, to't, to't, I say, and do not idle time. Come, Minstrels, play away, efaith my dancing-days are not done yet.

[Musick plays, they dance, at the end of which **WELLMAN** speaks.

WELLMAN
Friendly, you're out.

FRIENDLY
Death, you lie!

[Strikes him, he draws, they pass, the Company puts in all but **MR SHATTER** & **SIR JOHN**, who run in corners.

SIR LYONELL
The Quarrel, Gentlemen, the Quarrel! efaith, here's fine doings!

FRIENDLY
Oh, Sir, you have the advantage of the place.

WELLMAN [Whispers]
I do believe I have; and you're not safe here: I'll meet you, Sir, anon.

FRIENDLY
Do so. Farewel.

MARINDA
For Heavens sake, Sir, come back—what wou'd you do? if there be ought that you take ill from Wellman, declare it here, and let us end the Quarrel. I know 'tis some mistake; I know he loves you: let not a trifle set such friends at odds. Speak to him, Sister.

DIANA
Why how now, Sir, is this the proof you give me of your Love! Oh you have shew'd your self a gallant Spark! I thought it Jealousie, and took it kindly your rudeness to our Knight here; but to a friend, at least the man you call so, gives me some cause to fear you're angrie at his Contract with my Sister. Be friends, or I'll believe so.

FRIENDLY
Do so, I care not.

DIANA
Hah! do you not love me? Do not make me serious, I shall be out of humour if you do; and Heaven knows what a strange thing I may prove then; I never tri'd it yet.

FRIENDLY
I care not; pray unhand me.

DIANA
I will, in spight of all that wou'd detain thee. I never found my self thus much concern'd.

SIR LYONELL
What sudden flaw is this?

WELLMAN
By Heaven, I know not, Sir, unless some hidden flame for thee—

MARINDA
It cannot be, I never saw a glance, a look, or smile, cou'd be suspected Love: 'tis some old Grudge. Dear, do not follow him, my heart presages something that is fatal.

[Weeps then To **SIR LYONELL**.

Good Sir perswade him.

SIR LYONELL
Away, ye fool, perswade him not to fight! away, a Coward! hang't, he were not worth thy love then.

WELLMAN
Honour, my Deer, obliges me to go. Wou'dst have the man that has thy heart in keeping, be pointed out for Cowardize? Away, thou needst not fear, we shall at most onely exchange a Wound. Thy sacred Image guards my heart entire, and keeps it safe from danger. Go to the Banquet, entertain the Ladies, and be merrie.

SIR LYONELL
By Cocks bones shall she, and be very merrie, to think she's like to have so brisk a Spark to her Bed-fellow. Go thy ways, William, and God's blessing go with thee, Boy: if thou wants a second, I can push yet, I'm not so old efaith.

WELLMAN
I humbly thank ye, Sir; we shall think better on't perhaps before we fight.

DIANA
Or shall Sir John go? he's a man of mettle, I assure you, Brother.

SIR JOHN

What the Devil do ye mean! I have mind to take this opportunitie to be with thee, thou little wanton—

FRIENDLY
Fear not, Sir, I'll excuse ye.

[Goes out bowing to **MARINDA**.

SIR JOHN
You little amiable mischievous Ape you, what a scurvie malicious Jest did you break upon me, to make the Proverb good, You had rather lose your Friend than your Jest?

DIANA
A Jest! it was a parlous true one then: I said you were all Mettle; A brazen face, a leaden brain, and a copper nose and beard.

SIR JOHN
Wit, Lightning, and Quick-silver, thou little more than Dwarf, and something less than woman.

DIANA
A Wasp, a Wasp! Your Wit stings, Sir.

SIR JOHN
Thou'rt plaguie sharp; pray God thou be'st not too far gone in Love; if thou shou'dst, I must be forc'd in honour to marrie thee, tho introth 'twou'd be hardly brought about.

DIANA
No matter, Sir; things got by strugling, bring the greater pleasure, when dull Consent but palls the Appetite. Then thou'rt a fool too, the most admirable necessary for a Husband in the whole Creation, and the best Block to carve a Cuckold in.

SIR JOHN
Whe, what a tart Monkey's this! By my troth if thou hadst not so much wit, I cou'd finde in my heart to take thee for better for worse; for I finde thou con'dst bear me with all my faults.

DIANA
Bear with thee! I wonder how thy Mother bore thee nine whole months about her, when I'll be sworn I can scarce endure thee in my sight an hour.

SIR JOHN
Alas for you, sweet Soul, good lack! A pox of your Wit: By the Lord Harry, you are the proudest, scoffing, scurvie, idle, fantastical, whimsical—Ads nigs, because you have read St. George for England, Amades de Gall, and the Legend of Lyes, you are licens'd, forsooth, to abuse all the world: Egad, Sir Lyonell, your Father shall know't.

[Offers to go out.

DIANA

He must not tho—Nay, do not go in Rancor, good dear Knight; for I must confess a secret to you; which if you knew my heart, you wou'd believe there were nothing so cruel there as you imagine. I speak very kinde things of you between my Maid and I anight as I am going to bed, and next my Prayers too, Heaven forgive me! I spoke things of you that I wou'd not wish you shou'd know.

SIR JOHN
Nay, look ye, for my part, if I have not most religiously vow'd my heart yours, been drunk twice a day to your health, swallow'd Fire and inches of your Cuff-strings, eat Candles, pledg'd your health in Chamberlie, run Pins into my Arms, and done all manner of gallant and heroick actions, I'm the veriest son of a Whore breathing; and yet to tell me after all this, I have a brazen face, a leaden brain, and a copper nose,—

[Weeps.

—'tis most intolerable, insupportable, and prodigious, I'll be sworn.

DIANA
And de ye love me so indeed?

SIR JOHN
Love you! 'Sbud, whosoever says I do not, and honour you too, Egad; nay, and if you wou'd, wou'd marrie you, is a son of a Whore, and a Scoundrel, by the Lord.

DIANA
And let me tell you in return, that—Heaven forgive me! And my Sister knows I have took drink and slept upon't, that if ever I marrie, it shall be you; and I will marrie, and yet I hope I do not say it shall be you neither. Come, let's to the Banquet.

SIR JOHN
Oh, dear Creature, I do not say you do: Lord, how was I mistaken in thy heart! But will you hereafter cast a kinde look at me, to put me in countenance before Companie? That I wou'd be at now.

DIANA
Much may be done. Come, let's to the Banquet.

SIR JOHN
And will you, my prettie little Darling of mine eyes, marrie me? As I hope to breath, my Purse, Bodie, Soul and all, shall be thine.

DIANA [Aside]
Most affectionately spoken! Well, get my Fathers consent, and as for mine—the Devil take me if ever thou gets it.

SIR JOHN
A Kiss, and 'tis a Match.
Thus Hymen shou'd begin;
A falling out, sometimes proves falling in.

[Exeunt.

[Enter **WELLMAN** and **FRIENDLY**, as in the street.

WELLMAN
Well, my dear friend, tell me with open heart, hath not my Reasoning reclaim'd thy Folly, preserv'd thy falling Vertue, and secur'd it?

FRIENDLY
There is no Vertue in Blood, no Reasoning in Desire: But shall I not in this fond act of Love, do that which will to thee render my name abhorr'd, and make thee hate me?

WELLMAN
By Heaven, no.

FRIENDLY
And shall I then? may I enjoy Corina?

WELLMAN
Thou shalt, by all our Friendships. Here, take this Ring, shew it to that fair Devil, it will confirm me dead; which rumour, with my absence, will make good—Possess thy Love, grow wearie in her Arms, then be thy self again.

FRIENDLY
But if Report grows strong, and I am seiz'd, where shall I finde thee?

WELLMAN
At Glistens my Goldsmith in Cheapside, to whom I'll tell our business and designe.

FRIENDLY
Thither I'll come and tell thee how I thrive. Till when, farewel.
Goes out.

WELLMAN
When woman's in the heart, the soul's all hell. Now Repentance, the after-clap of Fools, light on thee; I have an Art left that may reclaim thee yet. I'll make thee fall into the vilest dangers, even worse than womans Lust. No Goldsmith will I see, or tell my storie to, but in some fit disguise I'll hide my self impossible to be discover'd, and leave thee to two friends, a Whore and Law, that will be plague sufficient for one man; but is this friendship in me?
[Pauses]
No matter:
No man is purely vertuous, no Vertue purely kind;
The end being good, the way is well design'd.

[Goes out.

SCENE II

SCENE: Changes to Corina's house.

Enter **CORINA** in anger, followed by **TRICKWELL** with Plate, and **MRS DUNWELL**.

CORINA
Oh, impudence, am I then fallen so low to be sollicited by Pimps and Panders! Hell take the trade, if this be the effects on't.

TRICKWELL
Madam, whatever you may think of me, my Present has the shew of Qualitie; here's Plate, a Present that a Lord might make ye; and I was once a Gentleman, tho I am fallen so low by faithless Vice, yet tho undone, poor and depriv'd of all, I have a heart and will, that still remains, and fain wou'd venture on when Beautie calls. And if I have a stock, which Heaven and my own industrie has lent, I must employ it still to that dear use. Take first this little Tribute of my conquer'd heart; I may in time increase it: were it Crowns, here they shou'd all be offer'd.

CORINA
And thus I'd spurn away: Base servile Villain, who livest by Noise and Riot, spunging upon the drops that fall from Gentlemen, canst thou believe that after Wellman's love, I cou'd receive a Raskal to my Arms?

TRICKWELL
If I were there, you'd finde but little difference; and possibly the next they entertain may fail to pay this price I offer ye. This Raskal and that beautious haughtie thing, bating the Sex, differ but very little. I live by Brauls, by rapine, and by Spoils, in Fears, Vexations, Dangers, so do you; I eat when I can get a fool to treat me, and you can do no more: Pox of your pride, methinks we two might understand each other; you've no Gallant to take your Quarrels up; you raign'd when time was, and I'll do so now, for you have known my love, shall finde my power, tho yet I nere durst tell you so.

CORINA
Nor shall not yet; for tho that Lover's gone, who but to look on wou'd have made thee tremble, I've Beautie still that may command another Beautie whose very glance shou'd make thee bow: Gods! and has it lost its awe?

TRICKWELL
It has, and I'm resolv'd upon a Conquest.

CORINA
Death, Sirra! stand off, and view my fatal hand, it carries death to the bold Ravisher, that dares approach unreverendly. A Whore! what tho to her that bears it 'tis a shame, an infamie that cannot be supported? to all the world besides it bears a mightie sound, petition'd, su'd to, worshipp'd as a God, presented, flatter'd, follow'd, sacrific'd to, Monarch of Monarchs, Tyrant of the world, what does that charming word not signifie! And darest thou raise thy hated eyes so high to gaze on such a Constellation! No, be gone, with all thy base-got worthless Trifles, quickly pack up, and hence, or I will kill thee.

[Goes out.

MRS DUNWELL
So, Sir, you had better have lookt no higher than Mrs. Mary Dunwell, who can down with you when money's low; but when once a little in Pocket, you are for high feeding, forsooth. Go get you gone, I may chance take pitie on you when her passion's over, and do you some service.

TRICKWELL
No, by Heaven, I'll try my chance this very minute, throw my last Cast, for the great Stake is set, and will enjoy her now.

[Goes in and knocks.

MRS DUNWELL
Hah! here's somebodie I hope will interrupt you.

[Opens the door.

[Enter **WELLMAN** disguised.

What wou'd you, Sir? wou'd you have ought with me? A proper handsome fellow, but ill drest.

WELLMAN
Madam, I am a Gentleman grown poor, decay'd by fortune, and wou'd gladly serve: I can obey, cou'd you direct me where.

MRS DUNWELL
This fellow wou'd serve my turn most admirably! but if I cou'd—you wou'd grow proud with feeding well and clean Linnen.

WELLMAN
I am not bred so ill, but I can tell how to be grateful to you.

MRS DUNWELL
Introth he apprehends most discreetly—but you're too big to wear a Liverie.

WELLMAN
Not at all; 'tis the fashion now for Ladies to keep tall men in Liveries: your Page is out of fashion, and your stripling Footman.

CORINA [Within]
Help! help! undone! Oh help!

WELLMAN
Hah, what noise is that!

[Draws, and runs in.

MRS DUNWELL

Heavens! the Rogue sure was ravishing her.

[Enter **WELLMAN** dragging in **TRICKWELL**, **CORINA** follows disordered.

WELLMAN
Damn'd sawcie Villain, what was thy pretence?

TRICKWELL
What's that to thee, bold interrupting Slave, sent by the Devil to hinder my delight?

WELLMAN
Dog—

[Going to kill him.

CORINA
Hold, do not kill the Raskal; 'tis enough you've sav'd me from his mischiefs: pray let him go.

WELLMAN
'Tis pitie, but I will obey. Take that, and that, that, ye Mungrel Cur; Dogs shou'd be us'd so.

[Kicks him out.

Death! what a very wretched thing's a Whore, that every Raskal dares approach with Love!

CORINA
Who are ye, pray, to whom I'm so oblig'd?

WELLMAN
One that wou'd gladly serve in any qualitie.

CORINA
I'll do thee good; take that.

[Gives him money.

I will prefer thee to some man of Qualitie: Mean time make this your home.

WELLMAN [Aside]
I wonder whether Friendly has been here!

MRS DUNWELL
Madam, one knocks; shall any have admittance?

CORINA
Onely false Wellman's Friendly. You may retire, and wait my farther pleasure.

[Exit **MRS DUNWELL**.

WELLMAN
I'll over-hear ye too.

[Exit **WELLMAN**

[Enter **DUNWELL** and **FRIENDLY**.

FRIENDLY
Now, my dear Mistriss, Soul of my desires, I come with all the Spoils of conquering Love, to lay 'em at thy feet. My Stop is dead, the Stop of all my ravishing Happiness; and here's the witness of my Victorie.

[Kneeling presents her the Ring.

CORINA
Dead! Wellman dead! Oh thou inhumane friend, that borest that title onely to betray him! Dead! and by thee! Heaven, can you let him live! Support me, or I fall to earth with this sad killing news.

[Seems to faint.

FRIENDLY
Heavens, Madam, what d'ye mean? or shall I vow to you he is not dead?

CORINA
Hah! not dead!

FRIENDLY
What wou'd you have me do? When I confirm him dead, you grow inrag'd; and when I say he lives, you kill with frowns.

CORINA
Traytor, and hast thou then deceiv'd my hopes? and is not Wellman dead? Hell, what is man! how didst thou swear, how didst thou prostrate lie, and beg'd to give me any proof of thy false Passion? I ask'd thee this; and is it thus you give it! Oh for a quick revenging Power to kill thee!

FRIENDLY
Calm that dear angrie face, and tell my Love which way it best shall please.

CORINA
Is't in thy choice, perjur'd, forsworn, and false, to tell me either? Damn thy double Tongue, and all this Beautie that mis-led thy truth, if thou hadst ever any in thy soul.

FRIENDLY
Then since it is my destinie to offend, which way soere I take I'll follow truth, and tell you, Madam, all your strict Commands I did obey, and Wellman is no more.

CORINA

No more! why what hadst thou to do with my Commands? Oh thou hast kill'd all that my soul cou'd love! Tho I commanded, yet he was thy friend, and that in generositie shou'd have sav'd him. Go from my eyes, far from my thoughts remain.

FRIENDLY
Is this then the reward of all my Love? What have I done, but been obedient? Had I priz'd my Friendship above that Love, wou'd you have took it well? Yes, I will be gone, and to the judging world
Prove who's the greater Criminal you or I:
I kill'd a Friend, you make a Lover die.

CORINA
I must not let him go, till I'm reveng'd. Stay, I relent; Oh stay, and give my heart a little time to take leave of its old acquaintance, ere it go to make a new and unknown choice agen. Alas, I lov'd this Wellman, lov'd him dearly, more than my life.

[Weeps.

FRIENDLY
Why did you kill him then?

CORINA
Why, in my own defence; he gave the first, I fear the mortal wound.

FRIENDLY
Then think it just, and think of him no more, but of the dear reward you are to give for all my service. Come, will you not?

CORINA
I will; but you'll receive it decently, and not with hands distain'd i'th' blood of him that lately was so dear to me?

FRIENDLY
Still on that subject? do not put me off; I've left the business of my life undone, and had not power to go about my Pardon, so hastie for the dear reward I was; and is it thus you treat me?

CORINA
You'll finde me all you wish, give me an hours time to compose my self; and all this upon my brow is but a modest decencie; one hour of joy will chase it all away.

FRIENDLY
Do not you dally with me?

CORINA
No by Heaven, when you return I'll give ye your reward, and what you most deserve—a Halter 'tis, false and perfidious wretch.

FRIENDLY
Here, keep this Ring, and think each minutes absence is a long year in love. Farewel.

[Exit.

CORINA
Farewel, vain credulous treacherous fool, farewel. Mischief inspire me now with all your Arts; methinks the sight of this instructs my Soul in a most noble piece of Villanie: I will to fair Marinda with this Ring, and frame a storie of so cunning mischief, shall stab her through the ear into the heart. By Heaven, 'tis greatly brave, and I'll begin it: Then when this false believer does return, I'll be prepar'd for him—What, Hoe, who waits?

[Enter **DUNWELL** and **WELLMAN**.

WELLMAN [Aside]
Now what a Devil is this woman grown!

CORINA
My Hoods and Fan, and call a Coach immediately:

[Exit **MRS DUNWELL**.

—and you, Sir, I must beg to wait on me.

WELLMAN
Where ever you command.—This was happie!

[Exit **OMNES**.

SCENE III

SCENE: Changes to Sir Lyonell's house.

Enter **SIR LYONELL**, **MARINDA**, **DIANA** and **MAID**, and **SIR JOHN**

MARINDA
Nay, good Sir, be not angrie that I sent; I was afraid some harm wou'd come of it, and so I fear there is.

SIR LYONELL
And did no one hear of him?

MARINDA
None; pray Heaven he be well; my heart misgives me.

SIR LYONELL
Well, if he be lost, there's a brave fellow gone, and in a time the King had need of Souldiers; there's idle Husbands enough for you, Baggages.

DIANA
I have a little kind of a scurvie pain too, which I do not use to feel about my heart, for Friendly—but none shall see it in my troubled looks: not that I care who knew the loving secret, but I'll not be laught at.

SIR LYONELL
Leave your whimpering, do: Wou'd thou hadst a heart like thy Sister here. When wou'd she cry for a man thus?

DIANA
Faith, Sir, when I have as much need of a man as she, that is, when I want one, I cannot dissemble.

SIR JOHN
Look ye, Sir, she has need enough, and thanks to fortune she's provided for, with your good liking, noble Sir Lyonell.

SIR LYONELL
Come, Sir, let's have one Marriage well over, before we think of another. Wou'd we cou'd hear of these Sparks too; 'tis almost midnight: they might have staid till day-light, and have kill'd one another like Christians decently, not by dark, as Cats and Dogs worrie each other. I know not what to think on't.

[Enter a **BOY**.

BOY
Here's a Ladie in a Coach below desires to speak with you.

SIR LYONELL
A Ladie at this hour! she shall be welcome; old as I am, I'll not deny a Ladie.

[Exit **BOY**.

[Enter **CORINA** and **WELLMAN** disguised.

SIR LYONELL
I hope your business is with me, fair Ladie.

DIANA
'Twou'd be but ill dispatch'd then.

CORINA
I know not, Sir; first let me crave your name, or are you Father to the fair Marinda?

SIR LYONELL
I am, fair Mistriss, for want of a better. By the Mass she's very handsome!
[Aside]
This is the Maid you name.

CORINA

My time's but short, and what I have to say I must dispatch. Madam, you had a Lover once, Young Wellman!

MARINDA
Had! (good Heavens!) I hope and have.

CORINA
No, Friendly has basely kill'd him.

MARINDA
Oh wretched lost Marinda!

[Swoons.

SIR LYONELL
Look to my Daughter!

CORINA
Madam, look up; this great concern he merits not: 'twas pitie brought me here to undeceive ye; his Vows and Soul were mine, intirely mine.

MARINDA
Why didst thou call me back to life again, or say in pitie that you undeceiv'd me? If you knew Wellman false, why did you stay me? You shou'd have let me di'd, 't had been more charitable; but if, as you affirm, he lov'd you best, which I believe from that fair form of yours, whilst I remain I needs must love you too.

DIANA
This must be malice sure!

CORINA
Madam, do ye know this Ring? he gave it me, and told me such things of your tiresome Passion, as gave us cause of laughter all the evening.

MARINDA
I cannot blame him that he lov'd me not, when so much Beautie as appears in you, gave him permission to adore it: but methinks 'twas ungentile to make a sport of me; he shou'd have pitied follies he created: he lov'd me first; alas, I sought him not.
[Weeps]
Help me, Diana, for I feeble grow! To morrow shou'd have been my Wedding-day, now I invite you to my Funeral; bring Flowers and strow the way to my cold Grave, and lay me down in peace.

SIR LYONELL [Talks aside]
Lead her in, and be careful of her; but, Madam—

WELLMAN
I cannot hold, I must reveal my self;

[Going stops.

Yet stay, Heavens, shall I suffer her to die! so good, so gentle, and so sweet a Mistriss? Were there but three such women in the world, two might be sav'd.—Yes, I'll have patience yet to see the utmost that this Devil aims at.

SIR LYONELL
Confest it, said ye, Madam? and to you? on what Acquaintance, pray?

CORINA
He was in love with me; and seeing no hope of gaining me whilst Wellman was alive, he pick'd a Quarrel with him, and dispatch'd him, and vaunted of the Villanie to me. Please you to go where I'll direct you, Sir, he shall confess the Murder.

SIR LYONELL
Madam, I'll go; and you, Sir John must bear me companie.

SIR JOHN
With all my heart, Sir.

SIR LYONELL
Madam, your hand. Roger, go you to Mr. Constable, bid him be readie if I have occasion, and careful who passes the streets to night.

[Exeunt **OMNES**.

SCENE IV

Enter **MR DASHET** and **SAM**.

MR DASHET
Sayst thou, Sam, at one Mrs. Dunwell's house? whe, she's a Bawd.

SAM
Yes, Sir, or my intelligence is false. There lies a Ladie, Sir, with whom he's desperately in love; and having no purchase-money, 'tis thought, hires the Bawd at the price of's own bodie, to get the young Ladie, Sir: They call her Corina.

MR DASHET
Lord, Lord, what will this wicked world come to! And there thou sayest I may be sure to finde this villanous Trickwell.

SAM
He never lies from thence all day, Sir, as I am inform'd; 'tis now about his hour of departure, and this way he must come.

MR DASHET
Get ye home, Sam; I'll ene take Mr. Constable and a Watchman or two, and fall to searching. Get ye home, Sam, thou shalt have a new Sute for this, honest Sam.

[Exit **SAM**.

Well, if I catch the Rogue, he shall be hang'd in lousie linnen: I'll hire a Priest to make a Papist of him before Execution; and when he's dead, I'll piss on's Grave.—

[Enter **TRICKWELL** in a Cloke.

But stay, who comes here? this may be he.

TRICKWELL
Damn this Corina, this proud scornful Beautie, whom I must humble and enjoy. I know I am a Rogue not worthie of her love, a Raskal that have no one Good about me, but that I love: And this damn'd Bawd, to keep me to her self, disgraces me to Corina.

MR DASHET
Aye, aye, this must be he—Ware shaving, Sir: What ho, the Watch! the Watch!

[Takes hold of **TRICKWELL'S** Cloak.

TRICKWELL
Death! 'tis Dashit's voice!

[Gets from him, and runs out, leaving his Cloak behinde with **MR DASHET**.

Thieves! Thieves! stop Thieves!

[Runs out, **MR DASHET** after.

[Enter the **WATCH** after, met by **TRICKWELL**.

CONSTABLE
Who goes there? come before the Constable.

TRICKWELL
Death, you are a prettie fellow of a Constable, to represent the King's Person indeed! here's a Watch for the Devil! honest men are robb'd under your Noses. A Raskal in the habit of a Vintner set upon me, cri'd stand and deliver, in the Kings Highway; he wou'd have had my Purse, but that my heels sav'd it: Yet he got my Cloak of rich Camlet, I'll be sworn, new and fair this morning. If you light on him, seize him, and keep him in the Stocks till the Cloak will hang him.

CONSTABLE
Doubt not our diligence, Master, these dangerous times.

1ST WATCH

Something to drink, Master, we that take pains for the good of the Nation.

TRICKWELL
Honest men, watch and sleep not. Good night.
Goes out.

1ST WATCH
Well, Master, we must watch better indeed. Is't not strange that Knaves, Rogues, and Thieves, shou'd be abroad, and yet we of the Watch, Scrivenors, Exchange-men, and Taylors, never stir a foot!

[Enter **MR DASHET** running with the Cloak.

CONSTABLE
Who goes there?

MR DASHET
An honest man and a Citizen.

1ST WATCH
The Knave's drunk, and speaks Riddles.

CONSTABLE
Come afore the Constable; what art thou?

MR DASHET
A Vintner.

CONSTABLE
Bring him neer: Hah, what's here, the Cloak?

1ST WATCH
Oh, Mr. Vintner! is't you? Hold, a rich Camlet-Cloak; 'tis the same.

CONSTABLE
Oh thou Varlet, does not thou know the Wicked cannot scape the eyes of the Constable?

MR DASHET
What means all this? as I'm an honest man and a Citizen, I took the Cloak—

CONSTABLE
As you're a Knave, you took the Cloak; we are your witnesses for that.

MR DASHET
But, Neighbours, hear me, hear who I am.

1ST WATCH
A Thief you are, we know.

MR DASHET
My name is Dashit.

CONSTABLE
I, I, we'll dash ye: in with him to the Stocks there, and lock him fast till morning, that Justice Lackbrain may examine him.

MR DASHET
Whe, but heark ye—

CONSTABLE
Const.
Away with him.

MR DASHET
Mr. Constable—

CONSTABLE
In, I say.
Locks him in the Stocks.

MR DASHET
Am I not stark mad yet, not quite an Ass?

1ST WATCH
You may be in good time, in grace a God, Sir. Well, what wou'd this Citie do, if 'twere not for such necessarie Tyrants as our selves to ride the free-born Jades, and humble 'em?

2ND WATCH
Prithee hold thy prating, minde our duties, and let's go sleep in the fear of the Lord.

[Exit all but **MR DASHET** in the Stocks.

[Enter **TRICKWELL**.

MR DASHET
Who's there? So ho! so ho!

[To him **TRICKWELL** like a Bell-man.

I shall be mad, lose my wits, and then be hang'd. Who goes there I say? thou mayst approach without fear, I'm fast by the heels.

TRICKWELL
'Tis Dashit!

[Rings his Bell.

Maids in your Night-rails,
Look to your light Tails,
Keep close your Locks,
And down your Smocks;
Keep a broad Eye,
And a close Thigh.
Good morrow, my
Masters all, good morrow.

MR DASHET
A Pox of Eyes and Thighs! Whe, Bell-man.

[**TRICKWELL** comes to him, holds his Lanthorn.

TRICKWELL [Through the Nose]
Good lack, good lack, Mr. Dashit! whe, what does your Worship in the Stocks? pray come out, Sir.

MR DASHET
Out, Sir! whe, I tell thee I am lockt.

TRICKWELL
Lockt! Oh Men, Oh Manners! Oh Times, Oh Night! that canst not discern gravitie and wisdom, in one of the Common-Council too! Whe, what's your Worship in for?

MR DASHET
For? a Plague on't, suspition of Felonie.

TRICKWELL
Nay, an't be such a trifle, Lord, I cou'd weep to see your good Worship in this taking: Your Worship has been a good friend to me; and tho you have forgot me, I have found your Worship's doors open, and I have knockt, and God knows what I have sav'd; and do I live to see your Worship stockt?

MR DASHET
Hah! alas, honest man, thou knows me then: Prithee call the Watch, and let the Constable know who I am, prithee do; and here, I have some money about me.

TRICKWELL
'Tis more than I deserve, Sir; let me alone for your deliverie.

MR DASHET
Do so, honest Bell-man, and then let me alone with that Knave Trickwell.

TRICKWELL
Maids in your Night-rails, &c.
Crying and ringing.

[Going out, enter **CONSTABLE** and **WATCH**.

Mr. Constable, who's in the Stocks?

CONSTABLE
One Dashit, for a Robberie. Dashit he calls himself: dost know him?

TRICKWELL
Know him!—Well, Mr. Constable, what good have you done the Citie! Know him! a most notorious Thief; his house has been suspected for a Bawdie-house many a year; a harbourer of Cut-purses and Night-walkers; he has been a long time in the black blook, and is he taken now?

1ST WATCH
How? Burladie, Neighbour, we'll not trust the Stocks with him; we'll to Newgate with him to rights.

CONSTABLE
Well mov'd, Simon. Come, Sir, come, Sir, out with him.

MR DASHET
Oh, does your Raskalships know me now? I thought you wou'd know me in the end.

CONSTABLE
Yes, the end of your worship we know.

MR DASHET
Aye, here's an honest fellow can inform ye.

CONSTABLE
Yes, we thank him, he has inform'd us you are a Pimp and a Thief. Binde him fast, and to Newgate with him.

MR DASHET
To Newgate! why Bell-man, Rogue, Raskal? To Newgate, amongst the prophane Jesuits too? oh, oh!

[Exit the **WATCH** with **MR DASHET**.

TRICKWELL
So, thou art like to thrive in thy Knaverie: Roguerie prospers with thee. To morrow is the Sessions at the Old-baily; I'll make him shrink with fear, ere I have done. Cou'd I but be reveng'd on this Corina, I shou'd be prosperous indeed;
Some little Devil help me at a pinch at need.

[Exit.

ACT THE FIFTH

SCENE the First

Corina's House.

Table and Lights.

Enter **SIR LYONELL**, **SIR JOHN**, **CORINA** and **WELLMAN**, disguis'd.

CORINA
This is my Lodging, Gentlemen; where, if you'l please to wait a little, you shall both see and hear the truth of what I've told you.

SIR LYONELL
But, Madam, Did he tell you he had kill'd his Friend? tell you himself, 'tis strange!

CORINA
Sir, If you find I wrong him, let me dye. He came all breathless, panting to my Chamber, his Sword all bloody, pray'd me to conceal him, for he had murder'd Wellman.

SIR JOHN
Under favour, Madam, what quarrel had they, said he, 'tis a most rare Creature, I'm half in Love already.

CORINA
Innocently was the unhappy cause; they lov'd me, both were Rivals in my Favour, nor knew I which my heart inclin'd to most; Wellman had Wit, Youth, Gaity and good Humour, lovely, well made, fit to engage a heart; and Friendly too was handsom, very discreet, very Amorous, soft in his Language, modest in his Actions; and tho' their Charms were different, yet 'twas hard to say who was the greater Conquerour; so I by favouring both, made either jealous.

SIR JOHN [Aside]
S'bud, wou'd I had shar'd of that without the danger?

SIR LYONELL
But Wellman was to have married my Daughter Marinda; to morrow was the day.

CORINA
To please his Father, Sir, he made you think so, he has oft with sighs to me confess'd he could not love Marinda, I hope she will believe, and dye in rage, and then I shou'd lye contented in my Grave.

SIR LYONELL
I pity thee, in troth now; but he was such a Villain, that but for his Fathers sake I'd let him dye unreveng'd—but Sir Jeffery Wellman's my Friend, and therefore I'l be dispos'd by you.

[Enter **DUNWELL**.

DUNWELL
Madam, here's the Villainous man come—as gay as a young Bridegroom.

CORINA

Pray Sir retire with these Gentlemen into my Closet, and you shall hear he will confess the murder, and having witness, you may apprehend him, and do you the while prepare the Watch, and let 'em wait below.

WELLMAN
With what a Fury is a Whore inrag'd?

[Puts **SIR LYONELL** and **SIR JOHN** into the Closet, and **WELLMAN** and **DUNWELL** go out.

CORINA
So now my Revenge grows high, cou'd I but hang this Friendly, which I wou'd because 'twas Wellman's Friend, and make Marinda mad,
Oh! with what Joy I'd follow—for 'tis I
Must end the last Act of the Tragedy.

[Enter to her **FRIENDLY** fine.

FRIENDLY
Now, my Corina, now, my Heavenly Fair,
I come to take that Joy which from thy Eyes
I find thou wilt allow my panting heart—
And here upon my knees receive my Vow;
If ever I prove false to so much Beauty
May I be ever scorn'd by Men and Heaven!
Oh! the excessive Joy that fills my Soul
With thought of my approaching happiness.
Come, lets draw nearer to our bliss, thy Chamber—

CORINA
But stay—

[Draws him near the Closet.

FRIENDLY
Oh! do not kill me with that fatal stay.

CORINA
You have not told me yet how you kill'd Wellman.

FRIENDLY
Oh! name him not, some fit of Love or Rage will seize thy Soul at naming him, and ruin me. My dear Corina, Mistris of my Life, name him no more.

CORINA
Now, on thy Life, by all I hold most dear, now Wellman is no more, the repetition will be wondrous grateful. Prethee, how fell the perjur'd faithless man? tell it me o're agen, and I'll resign my self for ever to thy Arms.

FRIENDLY
Tell thee and take thee! Were each word Blasphemy, wou'd every Syllable betray my Life, I'de hast to utter it for that Reward: though I can tell no more than what I've done already—that we met at a Ball, prepar'd for the contracting of Wellman to Marinda; where I being out in a Dance, or I at least pretending so, I struck him, we drew, but being parted there, I challeng'd him out, and it being late, we fought i'th street, where I had th' Advantage of him and kill'd him.

CORINA
What did you with the Body?

FRIENDLY
Drag'd it into Fleet Ditch, with the next Tide to flote where Fortune pleas'd, and slew my dear Corina—

CORINA
You shall dye for't, fond easie Fool—

[Enter **SIR LYONELL**, **SIR JOHN**, and lay hold of him: **WELLMAN** from below with **OFFICERS**.

SIR LYONELL
Seize the Murderer, Oh wicked Villain, base and treacherous!

FRIENDLY
Base and perfidious Woman! hold off your hands, and let me ask this Devil, why she does thus.

CORINA
Ah fool! that cou'dst believe my Love so slight to let thee, live, that murder'd him I liv'd for.

FRIENDLY
Well ye Gods! you have reclaim'd my Wildness, and brought me back to man,—and now I see the Strong Deformity of sinful Passion.

SIR LYONELL
Come, Come, Sir, we came not here to talk, 'tis Morning already, carry him directly to the Old Baily, the Sessions is now, and let him be hang'd out of the way.

FRIENDLY
You've Reason Sir, and deserve this Usage, but yet unhand me—thus I'de been serv'd had I indeed kill'd Wellman! but Sir he lives, lives at his Goldsmiths, one Glister in Cheapside.

CORINA
Heavens! Lives! Lives to be married! Oh—

SIR LYONELL
We are not to believe that Sir, to Prison with him till. he can prove this true.

FRIENDLY
No rudeness Sir, I'll go unguarded—Death! what a vile, poor, degenerate thing, a Mercenary Woman is—

SIR JOHN
How, a Mercenary Woman? Where the Devil have I liv'd, and how past my time, I knew her not before—this is her Man—I must get acquainted with him,—Friend—a Word I pray.

SIR LYONELL
How Sir, this Woman set you on! nay then Mr. Constable, pray lay hold of her, and see her forth coming.

CORINA [Weeping]
With Joy, since Wellman lives, and lives to be perjur'd, no matter what becomes of poor lost me.

FRIENDLY
No Sir, let me instruct you, take my Word I am a Gentleman, and known to you, she shall be forth coming if there be an Occasion, tho' she be false she is a Woman still, a beauteous lovely Woman—come Sir I'll follow you.

[**DUNWELL** leads in **CORINA**.

WELLMAN [And looking on]
I've yet a little Pity on my Heart, and that forsaken Beauty I have ruin'd.

SIR JOHN
But Sir you do not mind me.

WELLMAN
Said you Sir?

SIR JOHN
I ask'd you Sir, who this Lady was, to whom I perceive you belong; whether a man may be welcome for his Money—you conceive me.

WELLMAN [Angryly]
Sir?

SIR JOHN
Nay Sir, I ask your Pardon Sir, no Offence I hope; I'am a Knight by Birth Sir, and have Sir, some sixteen hundred a year Sir, no contemptable Fortune for a Gallant.

WELLMAN
A Gallant Sir?

SIR JOHN
Whe yes Sir, a Gallant Sir, whe what a Devil, I speak no Treason I hope in the Lord.

WELLMAN
But Sir you do as bad, this Lady is of Quality, and has a Fortune too, or if she had not, she has Beauty sufficient to intitle her to be a wife.

SIR JOHN
Say you so Friend, I must confess I am very much taken with her Beauty, but that I have a sort of an Ingagement upon my Person, to Mrs. Diana now, but I like this better by much Sir; and if she can but clear her self of the Business of this Murder, and has but any reasonable Fortune—and I get my self off this Diana—

WELLMAN
Who is she Sir?

SIR JOHN
Sir Lyonel Worthy's Daughter Sir, a little learing Titt as any's in England.

WELLMAN
Sir to serve you, cou'd you help me to the Speech of her, I wou'd do much, and have some artful Cunning.

SIR JOHN
Help thee, whe I'll carry thee immediately man, but do't so, as she may be very willing to part with me—or else, poor thing, twill grieve me to disappoint her.

WELLMAN
I'll warrant you for doing that; and clearing this Lady, and securing you a Portion.

SIR JOHN
E Gad, and I'm a Man made then—come along thou shalt have a handsom Reward for thy Pains too.

[Exeunt.

SCENE II

SCENE: Sir Lyonell's House

Two Chairs, a Table.

Enter **MARINDA**, and **DIANA**, and **MAID**.

MARINDA
But Sister is't a Sin to hang one's self?
Is it a Crime to dye when Life's a Torment?
Methinks Heaven shou'd forgive it.

DIANA
Prethee leave these Disputes, ye make me sad,
A Humour that I hate, and yet for Friendly,
I've try'd to weep and sigh, and have attain'd to't
With very much adoe.

MARINDA
Oh thou art happy, wou'd I were unconcern'd,
An even brutal Temper that no Miseries
Cou'd touch, nor Mirth cou'd elevate.

DIANA
Call you that brutal, give me that solid one;
I hate your thin and unsubstantial Soul
That every ject or small Assault of Grief,
Breaks through and makes ridiculous Mirth and Rage,
For every petty accident: Give me a Soul,
A Humour that's in Grain, not one that
Fades like Colours in the Sun, and changes like
Your Cheeks now pale, now red, and tells the World
The Secrets of your Heart; and yet I must confess I'm
Griev'd for Friendly, for you know I lov'd him,
Yet not so much to whine or dye for him.

MARINDA
'Tis true, when I consider he was false, methinks I should not dye.

DIANA
Nay, as for that I think you are mistaken, I believe him true enough, and that was some insensed Mistris, some of his Family of Love, that envyed your Happiness only, and came to put you in Despair, and I believe Wellman is not dead, nor can I think Friendly cou'd be so base upon any account to kill him; he's virtuous, has some Religion in him, and much honesty, prethee be pacified; come sit, you have not slept to night, sit and lets sing to you, and I dare hold you my Diamond Pendants to fifty Guinneys Wellman is alive. Come Ample, sing a Song.

[Enter **WELLMAN** and **SIR JOHN** at the door.

SIR JOHN
Look ye, Sir, I have brought you in, now lay your lyes as close together as you please, do you my bus'ness, and no matter how: I must to the Sessions house this morning to give my Evidence against Friendly.

[Exit **SIR JOHN**.

[**AMPLE** sings a Song.

MARINDA
Away! I'll hear no more! I cannot sleep! Alas, there is no Musick like my sighs and grones; leave me, and let me go— to rest, and Wellman!

DIANA
Ample, she swoons, help, help—

WELLMAN
By your leave, sweet Creatures.

DIANA
Uncivil Sir, what are you?

WELLMAN
One that brings comfort: hah! the Lady dying! stand off, I have a Cordial in my Voice—oh! she's gone, curs'd be my Trial! See, 'tis Wellman calls.

DIANA
Wellman! ha, ha, ha! Sister, look up, he's here.

WELLMAN
She stirs, give her more Air.

MARINDA
How have I slip'd off Life! where am I, hah! in Heaven sure, and this is Wellman kneeling: Art thou an Angel there?

WELLMAN
I would not wish it yet, no; we have an Age to come in love e're we arrive to that.

MARINDA
You live then!
[Softly]
I shall dy with Joy else.

WELLMAN
Call back the Blood into thy paled Cheeks, thou Miracle of Women! I made this tryal only to secure my Faith, and I believe you love, and I am happy; by all that's good, I never was unjust; that Woman, that beauteous Sinner whom you saw, I've been to blame with, but you must forgive the Errours of my Youth.

MARINDA
I do! and her! and must love whom you've lov'd.

WELLMAN
I thank thy goodness, but it shall not need, hereafter I'll tell thee all my Life, but now my time is short, and I must yet remain in this Disguise 'till Friendly's Tryal's past; for he shall suffer to the last degree, for leaving thee, Diana, for another.

DIANA
And has he been so wicked?

WELLMAN
Yes, but is now reclaim'd, but 'twas but in obedience to your Commands, you'd have him try to lose his Maidenhead, and he forsooth fell desperately in love, but I'll return the Penitent into your Arms again.

DIANA
Faith Brother, I do love the Fugitive, that's flat: and if my Father please, will marry him; but he's for Sir John Empty.

WELLMAN
But Sir John Empty is not for you, his heart's ingag'd to this Corina, my quondam Mistris, she strikes all dead that look on her, and I'm to get your consent he may leave you.

DIANA
Alas! pray tell him tho' 'twill break my very heart; yet what must be, must be, Marriages are made in Heaven, and so forth.

[Enter **SIR JOHN** running.

WELLMAN
Let me alone: but see where he comes breathless.

SIR JOHN
News, news, news, news!

DIANA
Mackerel, Mackerel, Mackerel, fresh come ashore.

SIR JOHN
Whe, how now, Mrs. Marinda! whe, you look blith and brisk upon't.

DIANA
Whe ay, is not that better than louring, and pouting, and puling, which is troublesom to the living and vain to the Dead? for my own part, let my Husband laugh at me when I'm dead, so he smile upon me whilst I live: I love a chearful countenance in all conditions.

SIR JOHN
Ay, but to see a Woman whine, and yet the Devil a tear falls; mourn, and yet keep her cheeks full.

DIANA
Ay, there's the Devil.

SIR JOHN
And yet I was heartily afraid y faith that I shou'd a seen a Garland on that Beauty's Herse; but Time, Truth, Experience and variety, have great power over Woman-kind.

DIANA
Well Sir, but to the business, the News you were so big with?

SIR JOHN
Why, 'tis this: the Publick Sessions this day holden at the Old Baily has condemn'd poor Frank Friendly.

WELLMAN
Hah! Whe Sir, he offered to produce Mr. Wellman at one Mr. Glisters a Goldsmiths.

SIR JOHN
That's all one, when it came to the test Glister deny'd he ever saw or heard of him, and his own Confession hangs him without more witness, and with him Dashit the Vintner is condemn'd for Robbery, and several others.

WELLMAN
How? Dashit for Robbery? and was it prov'd against him?

SIR JOHN
Only shrewd suspicions, 'tis thought he'l have a Pardon: a Cloak was stolen, that Cloak he had. The Justice was in Drink that committed him, the Judges severe and in haste, the Jury hungry, and so the Knave was cast; but hang him, he has cheated me with many an unmerciful Bill: but, Lord, to hear his mone, his wishes, his curses, his prayers, and his ill-tim'd Zeal, by my troth, they wou'd have made a Comedy. But, Sir, the Lady, the poor Lady you serve, and who betrayed Friendly, is sent to Newgate; Well, I'll take my Oath 'tis a lovely Gentlewoman, 'tis a thousand pities; they say she must be try'd the next Sessions.

[**WELLMAN** joggs **DIANA**, and whispers.

DIANA
Let me alone for a neat and seasonable lye;—how Sir, a Lady, pray, who mean ye?

WELLMAN
She that was here, Madam, and gave an account how Wellman was kill'd.

DIANA [To **SIR JOHN**]
Heav'ns, his Sister! Mean you Wellman's Sister Sir?

SIR JOHN [Aside]
How, Wellman's Sister?

WELLMAN
Wellman's Sister, Madam?

DIANA [Aside]
Can you do less for an abandon'd Mistris than tell a handsom lye to get her a good Husband? Say 'tis so, or I'll make mischief.

WELLMAN
The Gentleman knows 'tis so: I told him she was of Quality.

DIANA
A very virtuous Maid; Heav'ns! that I had but a Brother that wou'd marry her, and take her part in defiance of the World! Nay Sister, we must in Honour visit her: poor Innocence!

SIR JOHN
Hah! Wellman's Sister? Whe, look ye Madam, tho' you have not a Brother, I wou'd have you to know you have a Lover, that will do as much to serve you as any Lover in Christendom, and as for marrying her, for your sake, Madam, and to do the Lady good, I'de venture as far as Hercules, de ye see, or Alexander the Great, that I wou'd.

DIANA
Most Heroically spoken, the Contents do almost break my heart, yet, Sir, to let you see I scorn to be out-done in Bravery, I'le—give you leave—to marry her; and I think that's a bold word.

SIR JOHN
Egad and so 'tis.

MARINDA
Nay if you are so resolv'd, and keep that Resolution, 'twill not be hard to bring the Lady off, so many Friends joyning to her party.

DIANA
For my part I'll dye to serve her.

SIR JOHN
And so will I in blood, now I'm set on't,

DIANA
Come then, without Delay let's visit her,

MARINDA
Where? At New-gate Sister?

DIANA
At New-gate: Oh let not that Word fright you, because so many have gone to the Gallows from thence! martyr'd Innocence does often dye where Thieves and Robbers do; a Gallows may be sanctify'd, why not a Prison? Come Sir John your hand.

MARINDA [To **WELLMAN**]
And Sir I must beg yours.

[Exeunt.

SCENE III

Great-gate.

SCENE: Changes to the Front of New-gate at the Grate **TWO** or **THREE PRISONERS**, one a beging, a Box hangs out.

[To them **SHAMROCK**.

[Begs in a low Voice, and crys the while.

1ˢᵀ PRISONER
Pray remember the poor Prisoners, the poor Prisoners, pray remember the poor Prisoners. ho, ho, ho!

SHAMROCK
Dam ye for a Son of a Whore, how sneakingly do you beg— Remember the Poor—ye meeching Bitch, is that a Voice to dive to the Bottom of a Usurers Pocket, and fetch out Money in despight of his harden'd heart?—Remember the Poor? Pox of your snivelling, stand by ye Dog, and let me come to the Grate.

1ˢᵀ PRISONER
Alas, Mr. Shamock, me thinks we should have little Stomach to beg, I hear our Reprieves are out of Doors, and they talk of a Warrant for Execution, so that we may be hang'd to Morrow.

SHAMROCK
Why you whining Cur, be hang'd to Morrow? whe then we have the more need to beg hard to day, that we may drink at parting; Sirrah beg me heartily and with a good impudent Grace, I'll beat out your Brains with your own Fetters.

1ˢᵀ PRISONER
Oh! hold, hold, spare my Life good Mr. Shamock.

SHAMROCK
So, I see thou bear'st a Conscience, and wo't not cheat the Gallows of it's due.

1ˢᵀ PRISONER [Crying]
Oh no Sir, I have too much Repentance to wish to dye so wickedly, as I have liv'd; I wou'd go out of the World like a good Christian however.

SHAMROCK
Was there ever such a chicken-hearted Son of a Whore? thou wert ever a lazy Rascal, and I remember when we were getting a painful Living on the Kings High-way, wou'dst sleep the while, yet wake to share the snack, and to be drunk for Joy of the Prize: Stand away and observe me now, with what a laudable Voice I'll move Compassion:

[Pulls off his Periwig, turns his Cravate behind, thrusts out his Head and begs in a canting Tone.

Christians pitty the poor Prisoners of this loathsome and dismal Dungeon, and 'twill be restored unto you in tenfold; drop your Bounty into this little Box, the only Support, Relief, and Comfort of twenty wretched Souls.

[Enter **SIR LYONELL**.

Noble Sir, Remember the poor Prisoners:

[Enter **PARSON**.

[He pulls out a long Purse and puts in a two-pence.

The Lord reward your noble Charity, and restore it to you forty and forty fold.

[Pulling up the Box.

—'tis an old Oliverian two-pence, a damn'd Commonwealths pair of Breeches, confound the mark and your good Worships Bounty, was this all the large Lethern Purse and your more large Conscience cou'd produce, wou'd I were worthy to have a Dive or two at your reverend Pockets, I wou'd ease 'em for you with a Pox.
Hah! Ladies alighted—

[Begs again.

Most beautiful Ladies, dispense your noble Charity amongst twenty miserable Wretches, opprest with Hunger and Cold: Merciful and fair—pity the Miseries of unfortunate young men; whose few short hours of Life they've left, shall be imploy'd in Prayers for you our noble Benefactors: Oh remember the Poor!

[They give 'em Money.

Sweet Lady, Heaven reward your Beauty with eternal Bloom and numberless Adorers.

[Pulls up the Box, they go in.

Hah Gold! 'tis Gold by Jove.
Nay, now a short Life and a merry, we'l have it all in drink Boys, and when the Hour comes, dye like Hero's, sing the Psalm merrily, and then—be hang'd till we're sober.

1ST PRISONER
Ah! Mr. Shamock 'tis a long Nap we shall take e're we wake again.

SHAMROCK
No matter, then we shall not be dry next Morning.

1ST PRISONER
Oh this is sad jesting—Oh, Oh, Oh!

SHAMROCK
Here's a cowardly Rogue, now Plague on him, he's a shame to the noble Function of Padding: Sirrah, you shall have no Drink, 'tis thrown away upon the Rascal.

3RD PRISONER
Drink? rot him, let him lap salt Water from his Eyes, like a mangy Dog as he is.

SHAMROCK
Come, come, lets in and drink.

[Enter **KEEPER**.

KEEPER
Mr. Shamock, you must come down to your Devotion, here's a Parson come; Mr. Ordinary's sick; come away.

SHAMROCK [Sings]
Pox o' your Ceremonies, a man cannot be hang'd in Peace for your Parson, and your paultry praying— but come, hang't since we must obey silly Customs, let's down, and then—to drink, my hearts—go, get ye down.

[Exeunt.

SCENE IV

SCENE: The inside of the Prison.

Enter **FRIENDLY** in Irons, with **SIR LYONELL**, **MR DASHET** in Irons, **MRS DASHET** weeping by him, and others: **TRICKWELL** disguis'd like a Parson, seeming exhorting 'em: **CORINA** and **MRS DUNWEL** snivelling.

FRIENDLY
No Sir, I do not blush, nor are my cheeks grown, pale, tho' I'm condemn'd to dye a shameful death.

SIR LYONELL
No kind of Death is shameful but the Cause.

FRIENDLY
Which I well know is none, Heaven is my witness, none.

TRICKWELL
Ah! you are happy Sir!—happy to quit the World in Innocence, for Innocence—is a most heavenly thing—for Sir, Innocence is all in all; Innocence is—

[Picks both their pockets.

FRIENDLY
Very impertinent in your mouth, Sir,—you ought to have the manners to believe a dying man has other bus'ness—than to give ear to what you say; go preach to the Rabble, Sir, I'm not at leisure.

TRICKWELL
Ah!—what is sinful man—speak to him, Sir, to think upon his Soul, his precious Soul; ah, his too precious Soul—

FRIENDLY
Perhaps I'm not of your perswasion, Sir.

TRICKWELL
Hah! Heaven forbid—I hope you'r not a Papist Sir.

FRIENDLY
If I am, Sir, what then?

TRICKWELL
What then? whe then Sir, guilty or not guilty, you deserve to dye, and I'll prove it, and stand to't.

FRIENDLY
Prethee leave us, we are serious.

TRICKWELL
Leave yee, yes faith, 'tis time: you are not worth a Groat.

FRIENDLY
But is there Sir no hopes of a Reprieve?

SIR LYONELL
I'll warrant you Sir, I've Interest enough for that.

FRIENDLY
Upon my Honour, Sir, Wellman is but mislodg'd, and I've already satisfied yee how I came to say what I did of his Death to that fair false one,—sure some Lethargy has seiz'd him, that he appears not, or else he's mad, it cannot be unkindness, and it wou'd grieve you, Sir, to see me dye, and after find me innocent.

SIR LYONELL [To **CORINA**, who stands sullenly by]
By th' Mass, and so it wou'd, Sir; therefore I'll to Court about your Reprieve immediately; nor need you doubt my Diligence or Success;—but why, thou beauteous Hypocrite, didst thou betray him thus?

CORINA
I will not answer thee: I own my guilt, and am asham'd and angry at my Destiny: Were Wellman dead, I could endure the rest, but would not live to see him live another's.

SIR LYONELL
Well Sir, fare ye well till anon.

[Go's out.

FRIENDLY
Oh! how I hate what once I so ador'd!
He that's born well, and Nobly Educated,
Blest with an honest Fame, and worthy Friend,
And wou'd with desperate over-sight love all.
And land himself upon this fatal shore,
Let him ne're kill, or steal, but love a Whore.

[Enter **WELLMAN**, **MARINDA**, **SIR JOHN**, **AMPLE** and **SHATTER**, **DIANA**.

—hah!—what do I see?
Now everlasting Darkness cover me
From that dear injur'd killing sight, Diana.

DIANA
Nay, do not hide your Face, or turn away—I'm wondrous glad to know where a Maid may find ye when she has need of you; and tho' these Chains are something easier than those of Matrimony, yet, like a malicious Woman, I am for proposing a change; faith, what d'ye think on't? dare ye venture? methinks 'twere no ungrateful Leap from the Gallows into a fair young Ladies Arms?—wou'd you not rather cry, Drive away Carman?

FRIENDLY
Oh! do not mock my miseries, Diana!

DIANA
By this hand, not I; You may remember, I swore never to marry, till the man I lik'd cou'd give me proofs he was a man; you bow'd, and blush'd, and talk'd of Maidenheads, and modestly protested your Virginity; oh, filthy in a man! a man of sense too!—but you'r improv'd, I hear, grown wise of late, and given me proofs you are no Block-head; and I, to keep my word, am come to challenge you;—and to put you out of all these hanging apprehensions, know Wellman's alive.

[**WELLMAN** discovers himself, they embrace.

SIR JOHN
How! Wellman alive?

FRIENDLY
My dear, unkind, have you dealt well with me?

WELLMAN
I was resolv'd I wou'd be quits with you for getting my Mistress from me; which by the way I beg you wou'd forgive. I've a Design to marry her to Empty.

FRIENDLY
She is a Woman, and I scorn to injure her.
—And can you, Madam, except this Criminal in Chains?

DIANA
The sooner for that reason, with my Father's leave, I have a good hank upon you when you're insolent, to upbraid ye with the place from whence I had ye.

MARINDA
He cannot but commend your Passion for him.

FRIENDLY
I am asham'd to be so much oblig'd.

MARINDA
Nay, leave the shame to her.

DIANA
Shame, I laugh at it, and wou'd have believ'd none to have marry'd Friendly under the Gallows—therefore take my hand, and bind the bargain.

FRIENDLY
Thou art a Noble Creature, and I am thine for ever.

WELLMAN
By Heaven, Corina, it was not want of Love, my Fortune did depend upon my Marriage, but when I saw the Woman destin'd for me, I must confess I felt new flames possess me, without extinguishing the old, and I resolv'd to love her virtuously, and hold an honest Friendship still with thee—to raise thee up above the Worlds contempt, the fickle favours of unconstant man, and love thee as my Sister.

CORINA
What pow'rful Charms dwell in thy tender language! thou melt'st my rage with every softening look, and lead'st me a tame Captive to thy will;—I am still all thine, dispose me as thou pleasest.

WELLMAN
This Knight, Corina, then resolve to marry, I'll make thy Fortune equal to his Quality, the man is honest, young, and Master of himself. He thinks thou art my Sister—nor will I ever undeceive him.

CORINA
Well—since I must lose you, and am by your Commands obliged to Life, no matter how forlorn and wretched 'tis—

MRS DUNWELL
By my troth, Sir, you have left her like a man of Honour.

WELLMAN
Sir John, you are my Friend, and this my onely Sister, for whom I know you have a Passion; and since Mrs. Diana is dispos'd of, I am resolv'd you shall not be disappointed of a Lady. Take her, and trust my Friendship for her Fortune, 'twill not be inconsiderable.

SIR JOHN
Fortune Sir! I scorn she shou'd owe her Ladiship to any Fortune but what my single Honour can give. — therefore Madam, I am your Knight, your Champion, your most humble Husband and obedient Servant, John Empty, Baronet: but good Brother, let us make haste out of this scandalous place, it puts me so damnably in mind of mortality, it will spoil my Wedding-night.

WELLMAN
Ay Sir, as soon as Friendly's discharg'd.

MARINDA
You must give me leave to call—

[*This while* **TRICKWELL** *is seeming exhorting the* **PRISONERS**, *and picking their pockets,* **SIR JOHN** *and* **WELLMAN** *looking at* **TRICKWELL** *& the* **PRISONERS**.

—your Sister too, for I must love and serve all that love Wellman.

CORINA
Madam, the Generous Pattern that you have set me, I shall be proud to follow.

WELLMAN
Hah, Sure that Wench I know,—'tis she—whe how how now, Corina, what brought thee hither?

CORINA
'Fore Gad e'en my kind heart, Mr. Wellman, Love, villanous Love!

SIR JOHN
Hah, Love! whe, what a pox, is that become a hanging matter in our Age?

CORINA
If 'twere, your Neck's in no great danger.

SIR JOHN
Good Lord, what I warrant you think I was never in love then? yes faith have I, and have felt your Flames and Fires, and Inclinations, and Wamblings, as often as any He that wears a head.

CORINA
Then you are the first Fool I ever knew inspir'd.

WELLMAN
—spare him Corina, he's my Brother, but prethee say how came Love to bring thee to this fatal end?

CORINA
Fatal! 'tis my Glory—and egad my Statue and History ought to be added to the Gallery of Heroick Women—why you have hear'd I suppose, that my Husband was condemn'd last Sessions, Mr Shamock.

WELLMAN
What the famous Padder? is he thy Husband?

CORINA
Yes Faith, he had a Reprieve, but now the Warrant's sign'd for Execution, and he is to be hang'd to morrow.

WELLMAN
Well what's that to thee?

CORINA
Whe faith, we have liv'd lovingly hitherto together, and we'll e'ne dye as lovingly, for I am resolv'd to be hang'd honestly with him.

SIR JOHN
Honestly hang'd—how so?

CORINA
Whe I'll tell you Sir, when the Tidings came to me of poor Jack 's being apprehended, I soon knew which way the World wou'd go with him; I ne're snivel'd and nouted like a feeble Woman for the matter, but e'ne resolv'd bravely to take a Turn at Tyburn with him.

SIR JOHN
Lord have Mercy upon us.

CORINA
In order thereunto, what does me I, but hearing of a Fellow that had lost a parcel of Goods of value, but goes my ways to him, accuses my self for the Thief, was sent to Newgate, and to my great Joy and Satisfaction, was condemn'd with honest Jack efaith: On my Soul, Mr. Wellman, I trembled for Fear I shou'd have been acquitted, but the honest Jury took Pity on me, and brought me in Guilty. When the Devil wou'd any of your Wives of Quality have show'd this conjugal Constancy?

SIR JOHN
Lord deliver me, what a wicked World is this, that People shou'd have the face to confess their Villainies! she confesses all now, and some are hang'd and confess nothing.

WELLMAN
And wo't thou be so good natur'd to take a Turn with him at the Gallows?

CORINA
With as much Joy as e're I kiss'd him.

WELLMAN
Whe this is the most admirable Proof of Love, I ever heard off.

SIR JOHN
Proof of Love, proof of the Devil, Man, what to be slain at Tyburn for Love? whe 'tis most damnable and as nonsensical as to be hang'd for Religion.

CORINA
I find by your Principles that you'l keep out of Harms way.

SIR JOHN
Nay o' my Conscience, I shall ne're increase the Number of the noble Army of the Martyrs.

[Enter **SHAMROCK** chain'd.

SHAMROCK
Corina, where are you, here's the Fellow has brought home our Coffin.

CORINA

Let him bring't in my dear, you shall see Mr. Wellman, what a Device I have found out, never to part with dear Jack: I have bespoke a Coffin to hold us both.

SIR JOHN
How a Coffin? Lord have Mercy upon's, how great the Devil is with this Woman! but what care have you taken of your Soul all this while?

CORINA
That's the Business of Mr. Ordinary, he has so much a year allow'd him for managing that Affair, and has undertaken mine: Come bring in the Coffin.

[Enter **FELLOW** with a Coffin. They look on't.

SHAMROCK
Whe, what a Coffin's here? Is this a Coffin fit for Christians?—D'ye see, and all pitch't within too, ye Dog, we shall stick to't, a pox on ye for a nasty Son of a Whore.

SIR JOHN [To **WELLMAN**]
Bless me, sure these Reprobates never think of going to Heaven.

CORINA
Ay! I gave him two broad pieces in hand too, and two more I have in my Pocket to give him—

TRICKWELL [Aside]
Which I must be acquainted with.

CORINA
But he shall be damn'd e're he be so well paid.

SHAMROCK
Besides, Sirrah, you might have had the Manners to have lin'd it with a little Bays this cold Weather, but you have neither Conscience nor fore-cast.

SIR JOHN
Lord! Brother Wellman, I believe some Priests have been tampering with 'em, they are so wicked.

WELLMAN
Ha, Ha, Ha! a notable Observation.

SHAMROCK
I'de forgot too, I'll lay my Head to a Halter, this Coffin will not hold us both.

SIR JOHN
Hark ye Friend, don't lay with him, for he's oth' surer side.

CORINA
Yes my Dear, as for that I believe we may make Shift, 'tis but my laying my Arm under thy Head, and thou thine over my Breast, and we shall lye as snug these cold nights—

SIR JOHN
Whe the Devil's in these People.

CORINA
But I have a cursed Misfortune befallen me.

SHAMROCK
What's that, my dear Betty?

BETTY
The Whore the Laundress, who had all the Linnen I was to be buryed in, like an ungrateful Baggage, knowing I was to be hang'd, and she to have no more of my Custom, has pawn'd all, my lac'd Linnen too; so that, dear Jack, I shall come to thy Arms but scurvily equipt to morrow.

SHAMROCK
Lets arrest her. Lord, Lord, that People shou'd have no Conscience nor Honesty in 'em: what will this wicked World come to.

SIR JOHN
Ay! and to rob the Gallows too, unmerciful Tyrant.

[**TRICKWELL** comes up to her.

TRICKWELL
Young Woman, young Woman, this is no time to think of Trifles, and gew gaws; the best dress is that of Repentance, let your Conscience be clean and neat within, and no matter for Lace and Tawdrums; dress up your Soul I say.

[Picks her Pocket.

BETTY
Whe what a Pox have we here?

TRICKWELL
One who has preacht better Doctrine to your Ladyship e're now, and one who am appointed to put you in mind of your long home.

BETTY
Whe ye Fool you, have I been taking such pains to prepare my self for this Journey, and need your Advice in the Devils name? get ye gone ye canting Rascal, here's honest Jack can teach me how to dye worth a Legion of you formal Gown-men.

SHAMROCK
Gad thou'rt a noble Lass.

SIR JOHN
In Troth and so she is, 'tis Pity she shou'd be damn'd.

TRICKWELL goes to Dashet, Betty to the Joyner.

BETTY
Well Sirrah, here is your two pieces more, because I scorn to be worse than my word—

[Feels in her Pocket.

—hah! my money's gone—what's the meaning of this? I had 'em and the two pieces for Jack Catch too in my Pocket when I came down.

SHAMROCK
Whe what a Pox have we Thieves amongst our selves? this is fine doings efaith.

BETTY
Hang't let it go, they are some poor Devils that wanted it: go out and wait till I go up, and I'll pay you.

[Exit **JOYNER**.

SIR JOHN
Or let him call again to Morrow in the Evening.—

[**TRICKWELL** talking this while to **DASHET**, he making Grimaces to Wo, and crying and wringing his hands, **MRS DASHET** crying by him.

MRS DASHET
Well Husband, this is a very comfortable man.

MR DASHET
He is so. But, good Mr. Parson, leave my Soul a little while to it self, I pray, and let us have a little of your counsel concerning my Body. I owe Mr. Glister the Goldsmith 40 l. and suppose, Mr. Parson, when I am going to Execution he shou'd be so unneighbourly as to set a Serjeant upon my back—'twas for a Bowl—

[Bursts out into loud crying.

TRICKWELL
Ah! trouble not thy self, my Christian Brother with transitory matters, but have an Eye—an Eye I say to the main chance—

[Picking his pocket.

I'll warrant your shoulders; but as for your neck—Plinius Secundus, or Marcus Tullius Cicero, or some body says, that a threefold Cord is hardly broken.

MR DASHET [Crying still]
A very Learned man this—well, I am not the first honest man that has been hang'd, and I hope shall not be the last.

TRICKWELL

True Sir, therefore have a righteous Stomach: for you perhaps may sup in Heaven to morrow.

MR DASHET
Alas, Sin! I have no stomach to it at all Sir,—please you to take my Trencher, I never eat at night.

MRS DASHET
Ah, Husband, I little thought you shou'd have had need to have thought of Heaven so soon: oh!—had you been hang'd deservedly 'twou'd ne're have troubled me: for there's many an innocent man has been hang'd deserv'dly,—but to be cast away for nothing—oh,— oh.—

[Bawls.

TRICKWELL
Comfort your self, good Mistris, moderate Grief is decent, you'l shortly be a Widow, and I'm a Batchelor; I'll come and visit ye, and give you Christian consolation.

MRS DASHET [Crying still]
Ah, Sir! you shall be heartily welcome, and pray make haste.—oh—oh—

MR DASHET
Well,—I do here make my Confession before all good Christian People, and do declare—that if I owe any man any thing, I do heartily forgive him.

SIR JOHN
In truth, Religiously spoken. Whe, this is something.

MR DASHET
But—but, if any man owes me any thing, let him pay my Wife.

SIR JOHN
A good reason too y faith.

MR DASHET
There—are—the Writings of that Rogue's Estate who has brought me to this untimely End-dear Writings to me, God knows.

MRS DASHET
Where had you these?

MR DASHET
I took 'em out yesterday, thinking to have carry'd 'em to my Lawyers, in order to taking the forfeiture of 'em: now thou may'st do't.

MRS DASHET
Ay, ay, Husband, I'll warrant ye, I shall be diligent.

MR DASHET [Weeping]
And now, good Yoke-fellow, take leave of thy honest and true Dashet.

MRS DASHET [Cryes]
No, Husband, an't please the Lord I'll not leave you now,—I'll see you hang'd first—

TRICKWELL
Hah, my writings! now for a trick of dexterity to retrieve those, and I'm a man again—
[Aside]
—but Brother, you must remember your sins too, and iniquities; you must consider you have been a Broacher of prophane Vessels, you have made us drunk with the juice of the Whore of Babylon: for whereas good Ale, Perry, Syder, and Metheglin, were the true Ancient British and Trojan Drinks, you have brought in Popery, meer Popery— French and Spanish Wines, to the subversion, staggering, and overthrowing of many a good Protestant Christian;—oh! remember the Sins of the Cellar, beloved, the Mid-night sins that have been unsavoury to the tasts of your Customers, when you put the change upon 'em: remember your double scorings and long Bills, ah, remember your long Bills.

[This while he picks **MRS DASHET'S** pocket of the Writings.

WELLMAN [Aside]
This is that Rogue Trickwell.

MR DASHET
Ah! I confess, I confess, and forgive.
[Cryes]
—has any heard of one Trickwell?

TRICKWELL
Trickwell; yes, I know him well: a very honest Religious man, and an unright Dealer with his Neighbours, and their Wives speak well of him.

MR DASHET
I'll take it upon my Death he's the cause of my hanging, but I heartily forgive him; and if he wou'd but yet come forth and save me, I wou'd set him free from the Law, and discharge him for injuring me.

WELLMAN
And wou'd you from the bottom of your Soul forgive him all his cheats and Rogueries?

MR DASHET [Cryes]
I wou'd, and be bound in a thousand pound Bond to save him from the Law: ah! but 'tis impossible—

WELLMAN
Why look ye, Sir,—behold, your worshipful Friend and humble Servant Thomas Trickwell.

TRICKWELL
Hah! discovered by Mr. Wellman.

MR DASHET
Trickwell!

WELLMAN
Now bawling Mr. Dashet.

MR DASHET
Who wou'd have look't for a Wolf in Sheeps cloathing? or a Knave in a Parson's Gown?

TRICKWELL
No railing Dashet, if you do, I'l swear against you yet.

MR DASHET
Ay do, and damn your Soul.

TRICKWELL
What with a little Perjury? the Lord have Mercy on our Age then: No, no Sir, I'll retrieve you from the Gallows, but as for your Goods and Moneys it must go towards the use of my two hundred pound a year, which you have kept me from this two years, and of which now, thanks to my Dexterity, I stand again possest.

[Shows the Writings.

MR DASHET
How my Writings gone?

TRICKWELL
Thank God you're so rid of them, for I had been an eternal Rent charge upon you else, if I had not hang'd you: you know you had 'em for a little damn'd ballderdash Wine—

MR DASHET
Well, I'de better loose my Writings than my Life.

WELLMAN
Hold Trickwell;—yonder Woman I have been oblig'd to, and you have had Relief from—no Writings nor Pardon under marrying Mrs. Mary here—

[Pointing to **DUNWEL**.

TRICKWELL
Lord, Sir, what a Bawd?

WELLMAN
The better Sirrah, she has a good Calling then, when all fails.

MRS DUNWELL
Gods Blessing of your heart, Sir.

WELLMAN [Aside to him]
No grumbling, do't or I'le deliver:—remember Sirrah how you used my Mistress last night, and had the Impudence to rival me—

TRICKWELL
Well Sir of two Evils I'll chuse this—give me thy hand Moll, thou'st been a loving Soul I must confess.

MR DASHET
So there's some Revenge, I cou'd even cry for Joy now,

MRS DASHET
And so cou'd I top, if I knew for what.

[Enter **SIR LYONELL**.

SIR LYONELL
Here, where's Mr. Friendly—here's your Reprieve Sir, Hah! Marinda and Diana!

DIANA
Yet with their Husbands Sir.

SIR LYONELL
How, How?—hah! Mr. Wellman alive? and with Mr. Friendly—God bless ye, God bless ye all, I'm glad on't.

SIR JOHN
Ay Sir, and I am maryed to this Lady.

SIR LYONELL
I'm glad of that too.

[Enter **KEEPER** with a Reprieve.

Here Mrs. Betty, where are you? Here's a Reprieve come for you:

BETTY
Hah a Reprieve! What Devil ow'd me this malicious Spight, a Reprieve—dam thee, thou ill, thou ominous looking Dog, ever the Messenger of Hellish Tidings: Oh! I cou'd tear thy hated Tongue out—Rogue—

[Beats him.

SHAMROCK
Nay, dear, better be patient, and if we must part.—

BETTY
Art thou turn'd cruel too, and preachest Patience?
Patience with Life—no, I defie my Fate—
Scorning to live without thee thou shalt see,
I'll find a thousand ways to dye with thee.—

[Led weeping with **SHAMROCK** out.

SIR LYONELL
By 'th Mass a hearty Wench I'll warrant her, but come let's away: good Boys let's home and Dance, but first give Money to these poor Wretches.

[Throws his long Purse amongst 'em.

From this dire place many to Death have gone,
But to be marry'd, very rarely one.

Aphra Behn – A Short Biography

Aphra Behn was baptised on December 14th in 1640.

Although she was a prolific and well established writer in her own lifetime facts about her remain scant and difficult to confirm. What can safely be said though is that Aphra Behn is now regarded as a key English playwright and a major figure in Restoration theatre

In fact even where and to whom she was born are subject to discussion.

According to which account you read – and there are many – Aphra was born in Harbledown, near Canterbury. Another that she was born to a barber, John Amis and his wife Amy. Or again she was born to a couple named Cooper.

In the "The Histories And Novels of the Late Ingenious Mrs. Behn" (1696) it is written that Aphra was born to Bartholomew Johnson, a barber, and Elizabeth Denham, a wet-nurse. However a claim by Colonel Thomas Colepeper, who states he knew her as a child, wrote in Adversaria that she was born at "Sturry or Canterbury" to a Mr Johnson and that she had a sister named Frances. Anne Kingsmill Finch, Countess of Winchilsea, a poetic contemporary, says that Aphra was born in Wye in Kent, and was the 'Daughter to a Barber.'

None of these accounts can be relied upon and it follows that with so few facts the early part of her life cannot be clearly illustrated.

However what can be accurately suggested is that Aphra was born in the rising tensions to the English Civil War. Obviously a time of much division and difficulty as the King and Parliament, and their respective forces, came ever closer to conflict.

But still facts do not reveal themselves in any quantity. As a young woman a version exists of Aphra's journeying to Surinam with Bartholomew Johnson. He was said to have died on the journey, leaving his wife and children spending some months in the country. It is during this trip that Aphra claims to have met an African slave leader. These experiences formed the basis for one of her most famous works, "Oroonoko". In "Oroonoko" Behn Aphra gifts herself the position of narrator and her first biographer accepted the proposition that Aphra was indeed the daughter of the lieutenant general of Surinam, as in the story. There is little evidence to support this case, and none of her contemporaries acknowledge this, or any, aristocratic status. There is also no evidence that Oroonoko existed as an actual person or that any such slave revolt, is anything but an invention.

However it is possible that she acted a spy in the colony. Possibilities exist. Perhaps Aphra re-wrote her own history as and when it suited her needs at the time.

The common method of gathering information in these times was Church records and for a few, tax records. Aphra Behn is mentioned in neither. As well as Aphra Behn or Mrs Behn she was, at times, also known as Ann Behn, Mrs Bean, agent 160 and Astrea.

Shortly after her supposed return to England from Surinam in 1664, Aphra may have married Johan Behn (also written as Johann and John Behn). He could have been a merchant of German or Dutch extraction, possibly from Hamburg. He died or the couple separated that same year, however from this point we can be sure Aphra used the title "Mrs Behn" as her professional name.

There is some suggestion that Aphra may have been a Catholic or at least leaned towards this school of faith. She once commented that she was "designed for a nun." Many of those around her were Catholic, such as Henry Neville who was later arrested for his Catholicism, and this would have aroused suspicions during the anti-Catholic fervour of the 1680s. She was a monarchist, and her sympathy for the Stuarts, and particularly for the Catholic Duke of York may be demonstrated by her dedication of her play "The Rover, Part II" to him after he had been exiled for the second time. Aphra was dedicated to the restored King Charles II. As political parties emerged during this time, Aphra became a Tory supporter.

By 1666 Aphra had become attached to the court. Domestically the Plague was sweeping the Nation and the Great Fire was about to erupt through London. In foreign affairs England and the Netherlands had engaged in The Second Anglo-Dutch War from 1665. Aphra was recruited as a political spy in Antwerp on behalf of King Charles II, possibly in league with Thomas Killigrew.

This is probably the beginning of more accurate records on Aphra's life. Her code name is said to have been Astrea (though there are others), a name under which she later published many of her writings. Her chief duty was to establish a relationship with William Scot, son of Thomas Scot, a regicide who had been executed in 1660. Scot was believed to be ready to become a spy in the English service and to report on the activities of the English exiles who were thought to be plotting against the King. Aphra arrived in Bruges in July 1666 with a mission to secure Scot into a double agent, but there is evidence that Scot would betray her to the Dutch.

Aphra however found life as a spy not quite the romantic interlude that many assume would be the case. She arrived unprepared; the cost of living shocked her, and after a month, she had to pawn her jewellery. King Charles was slow in paying, either for her services or for her expenses whilst abroad. She had to borrow money so she could return to London, where she spent a year petitioning King Charles for payment unsuccessfully. A short while later a warrant was issued for her arrest, but little to suggest it was actually served or that she went to prison for her debt.

The death of her husband and her debts seemed to push her towards a more sustainable and substantial career. Aphra began work for the King's Company and the Duke's Company players as a scribe. These were, in fact, the only two licensed theatre groups in London. The theatres had been closed under Cromwell and were now re-opening under Charles II and a more liberal atmosphere.

Theatre technology was being imported from Europe and being integrated into the staging of some plays. It was a great moment on which to embark upon a career in theatre.

Aphra who had previously only written poetry now embarked on such a career. Her first, "The Forc'd Marriage", was staged in 1670, followed by "The Amorous Prince" (1671). After her third play, "The Dutch Lover", fails to please Aphra had a three year lull in her writing career. Again it is speculated that she went travelling again, possibly once again as a spy.

After this sojourn her writing moves towards comic works, which prove commercially more successful. Her most popular works included "The Rover" and "Love-Letters Between a Nobleman and His Sister" (1684–87).

With her growing reputation Aphra became friends with many of the most notable writers of the day. This is The Age of Dryden and his literary dominance. As well as his friendship she includes also those of Elizabeth Barry, John Hoyle, Thomas Otway and Edward Ravenscroft, and was also attached to the circle of the Earl of Rochester.

Aphra often used her plays to attack the parliamentary Whigs claiming, "In public spirits call'd, good o' th' Commonwealth... So tho' by different ways the fever seize...in all 'tis one and the same mad disease." This was Aphra's criticism to parliament which had denied the king funds.

From the mid 1680's Aphra's health began to decline. This was exacerbated by her continual state of debt and descent into poverty.

In 1687 she published A Discovery of New Worlds, a translation of a French popularisation of astronomy, Entretiens sur la pluralité des mondes, by Bernard le Bovier de Fontenelle, written as a novel in a form similar to her own work, but with her new, religiously oriented preface.

As her end approached in 1689 it became increasingly hard for her to even hold a pen though her desire to continue to write was unquenchable. In her final days, she wrote the translation of the final book of Abraham Cowley's Six Books of Plants.

Aphra Behn died on April 16th 1689, and is buried in the East Cloister of Westminster Abbey. The inscription on her tombstone reads: "Here lies a Proof that Wit can never be Defence enough against Mortality." She was quoted as stating that she had led a "life dedicated to pleasure and poetry."

Her legacy is broad. Firstly as a woman she broke down many of the barriers which regarded only men as writers, especially in the commercial arena. In all she would write and have performed 19 plays, contribute to more, and become one of the first prolific, high-profile female dramatists in these Isles.

In her own golden age of the 1670s and 1680s she was one of the most productive playwrights in Britain, second only to the immense talents of the Poet Laureate John Dryden.

Much of her work has been criticised for its bawdy tone as well as its masculine form but needs must and she was working to live, to survive, and to widen her spread as an author.

She received widespread support from many other successful writers including Thomas Otway, Nahum Tate (also a Poet Laureate), Jacob Tonson, Nathaniel Lee and Thomas Creech.

Aphra is now rightly seen as a key dramatist of the seventeenth-century theatre. Her prose vitally important to the on-going development of the English novel.

Following Aphra's death new female dramatists such as 'Ariadne', Delarivier Manley, Mary Fix, Susanna Centlivre and Catherine Trotter acknowledged Behn as an inspiration who opened up the public space for women writers to be accepted.

In succeeding centuries her appreciation has been volatile. For instance in the morally reserved Victorian clime both the writer and her works were ignored or dismissed as indecent. The Victorian novelist and critic Julia Kavanagh wrote, "the disgrace of Aphra Behn is that, instead of raising man to woman's moral standard, she sank woman to the level of man's coarseness".

However by the 20th century, however, Aphra's fame was back in fashion. Since then her works have been well appreciated and her place in our literary pantheon assured.

Aphra Behn – A Concise Bibliography

Plays
The Forced Marriage (1670)
The Amorous Prince (1671)
The Dutch Lover (1673)
Abdelazer (1676)
The Town Fop (1676)
The Rover, Part I (1677)
Sir Patient Fancy (1678)
The Feigned Courtesans (1679)
The Young King (1679)
The False Count (1681)
The Rover, Part II (1681)
The Roundheads (1681)
The City Heiress (1682)
Like Father, Like Son (1682)
Prologue and Epilogue to Romulus and Hersilia, or The Sabine War (November 1682)
The Lucky Chance (1686) with composer John Blow
The Emperor of the Moon (1687)
The Widow Ranter (1689)
The Younger Brother (1696)

Novels
The Fair Jilt
Agnes de Castro
Love-Letters Between a Nobleman and His Sister (1684)
Oroonoko (1688)

Short Stories

The Fair Jilt (1688)
The History of the Nun: or, the Fair Vow-Breaker (1688)
The History of the Servant
The Lover-Boy of Germany
The Girl Who Loved the German Lover-Boy

Poetry Collections
Poems upon Several Occasions, with A Voyage to the Island of Love (1684)
Lycidus; or, The Lover in Fashion (1688)

www.ingramcontent.com/pod-product-compliance
Lightning Source LLC
Chambersburg PA
CBHW051659040426
42446CB00009B/1220